Many in today's culture, even Christians, fail to understand the responsibility we have to handle God's resources effectively. As a result, we become poor caretakers of what our Lord has entrusted to us. In *Surrendering to Win*, Neal Broome challenges our complacency, our tendency to ignore our responsibilities, and calls us to carefully follow what Scriptures teaches us to do. Reading and listening to his wise instruction will bless you beyond measure.

PHIL WALDREP,
Phil Waldrep Ministries

. . .

Neal Broome has written a fantastic book on the life of a faithful steward. It's succinct, substantive, and practical. I've already shared some of Neal's advice with my three adult children. Get this book. Read it. Then apply it to your life. You'll be glad you did!

STAN BUCKLEY,
Founder and Executive Director of But God Ministries

. . .

The title of the first chapter, "Surrendered Stewardship," says everything about this book. I found the book to be compelling and challenging to my faith. It is well written and extremely practical. This may very well be a book that you want to read and reread. Neal obviously practices what he preaches, which makes what he writes very authentic. I recommend it highly to anyone who is serious about handling the resources that God has entrusted to them in a surrendered life.

RON BLUE,
Founder, Ronald Blue Trust

. . .

In *Surrendering to Win*, Neal Broome offers a practical, simple, biblical, radical call to live with a Kingdom mindset in our mixed-up world.

Dr. Chip Henderson,
Senior Pastor, Pinelake Church

. . .

Personal. Practical. Powerful. From our dash to our cash and from stewardship to leadership, Neal has offered a refreshing approach to these life defining principles. It seemed a contradiction when I considered the title of *Surrendering to Win*, but in life and in business, I have learned you have to give up to go up. We must be willing to give up on our plan so we can embrace God's best for our lives. In business we must be willing to delegate so we can elevate. I can't wait to pass this book on to my four adult kids and my wife because it has something to say to every generation.

Oscar Miskelly,
Founder and CEO, Miskelly Furniture

. . .

As a church stewardship pastor, I am thrilled with what Neal Broome has written in *Surrendering to Win*. Dealing with money is one of the few areas that impacts 100% of the population, yet is rarely addressed from God's perspective. A clear biblical theme teaches that our relationship to money impacts our relationship to God and it starts with surrendering our ownership and control to God's ownership and control. I wish every believer would read this excellent book and take these words to heart.

Dave Briggs,
Stewardship Pastor, Central Christian Church of Arizona

. . .

Surrendering to Win encompasses the very essence of stewardship, relinquishing control to a Heavenly Father. We are encouraged to give up our own will, recognizing our frailty and insufficiency to the One who is loving, infinite, and wise. As we surrender to an almighty God, we gain His strength as He becomes our undefeatable ally. Having been a believer for over 50 years, I wondered what I could learn in reading another book on surrender. Yet, Neal speaks from an honest, humble and Christ-touched soul to the heart of a man who wants more of Christ's touch. God has given Neal a unique gift for articulating this special message of surrender. May God use *Surrendering to Win* to refresh your commitment and life to Him.

DAVID J. MOORE CFP,
Sr. Financial Advisor, Compass Advisory Partners

. . .

Regardless of where you are on your walk with God, *Surrendering to Win* contains valuable insight for any man or woman in search of a stronger relationship with our Heavenly Father. Neal reminds believers that God is in control and encourages us to surrender daily to His will for our life.

MICHAEL GUEST,
Congressman

Surrendering to
WIN

Finding Victory through Biblical Stewardship

Neal Broome

 KINGDOM LIFE PUBLISHING

© 2021 by Neal Broome

All rights reserved. This book or any portion thereof may not be reproduced or used in any manner whatsoever without the express written permission of the publisher except for the use of brief quotations in a book review.

ISBN: 978-1-7362697-0-1

CONTENTS

Introduction 1
Chapter 1: Surrendered Stewardship 13
Chapter 2: Control Freaks 25

Section 1: *Our Time*

Chapter 3: Life Is Short 37
Chapter 4: Choices and Consequences 47
Chapter 5: Stewarding Time Wisely 59

Section 2: *Our Talents*

Chapter 6: Who Am I? 73
Chapter 7: Winning at Work 85

Section 3: *Our Treasures*

Chapter 8: Managing God's Money 99
Chapter 9: Radical Generosity 113
Chapter 10: The Prosperity of the Gospel 127
Chapter 11: Treasuring Relationships 141

Section 4: *The Gospel*

Chapter 12: The Greatest Surrender 155
Chapter 13: Is the Bible True? 169
Chapter 14: The Greatest Stewardship 183

Conclusion

Chapter 15: Creator or Creation? 199
Wrap-Up 209

INTRODUCTION

It is the most important word ever written in any book at any time. It only has three letters, but it is found in the very first verse of the very first chapter of the very first book of the Holy Bible. *God.* In the beginning, *God.* Not you, not me, not anyone else—God. There is a great God who created the entire universe. He is all-powerful and all-knowing. He always has been and always will be. He created the stars in the sky and the sky. He created the fish in the sea and the sea. From the dust of the earth, he created us. He holds the entire world in the palm of his hand.

Our finite minds cannot comprehend the power, beauty, and majesty of infinite, almighty God. If we want to embrace the Christian faith and allow its truths to transform our hearts, this is where it all begins. As Rick Warren stated in his best-selling book, *The Purpose Driven Life*, it is not about us. It all starts with God.[1]

If we are willing to pause long enough to ponder our existence, there simply is no other logical conclusion. I am a tiny blip on a giant radar screen. Things operated smoothly before I was born and will continue to long after I'm gone. Contrary to how we sometimes think and act, the world doesn't revolve around us. If you really need a "perspective adjustment" and want your selfish pride destroyed, I encourage you to watch Louie Giglio's sermon "Indescribable." God is big. Really big! Really, really big! And I am not. He reigns supreme as King. He is in control; I am not.

---

1 Warren, Rick. *The Purpose Driven Life* (Grand Rapids, Michigan: Zondervan, 2002).

Surrendering to WIN

This book is all about surrendering everything to our incredible heavenly Father, surrendering every area of your life to God and then stewarding your time, talents, and treasures in a manner consistent with God's perfect design. He alone can be trusted, and he alone is worthy of our complete and total devotion.

When I was a kid, there was a new line of action figures launched called Masters of the Universe. These strong men had large muscles and heavy battle gear and lived in mighty castles. My brothers and I would spend hours on the floor engaged in a good guy versus bad guy battle. As much as we enjoyed playing with these battle characters, my mom never liked them. To her, the name Masters of the Universe wasn't appropriate. She was right.

He-Man and Skeletor may have been the masters of this fake universe, but my mom knew who the master of the real universe was: God. The same God who created the entire universe. Are you ready for the cool part? All-powerful, all-knowing, almighty God isn't too big for us. As a matter of fact, he cares about every detail of our lives. He cares about our hurts and our fears. He cares about our dreams and our plans. He cares about our jobs, our money, and our hobbies. More importantly he cares about our relationship with him.

We are the crown of God's creation. We are the apple of God's eye. He created us in his image and breathed his very breath into us to give us life. God loves his children with a love we cannot even comprehend. We were made by him and for him. Since it's his breath in our lungs, what should our response be? To pour out our praise to him! (Someone should write a song about that.) Our chief purpose in life is to glorify God and enjoy a loving relationship with him and his creation. If you want your life to have meaning, begin living out that last sentence. When the greatest desire of your heart is to please God and deepen your relationship with him, everything changes. Your thoughts, words, and actions

INTRODUCTION

now pass through a different filter. Transformation occurs. Life is no longer all about you. "God owns it all" becomes a deep core conviction instead of just a cute Sunday-school saying.

Psalm 24:1 tells us that "the Earth is the Lord's and everything in it. The world and all who live in it." Do we really believe this? That the Lord owns the earth? And everything in it? That includes me and all my stuff. It includes you and yours too. A better question might be, do we *live* as though we really believe this? Let me say it again. God owns it all. He is over and above all things. This land is his land. We are simply pilgrims passing through at the time that he selected for us.

Despite being equipped with this knowledge, we still go through life as though we do not need God. We selfishly make life all about us. Our comfort, our convenience, and our cash accounts dominate our thinking when decisions need to be made. In many ways our affluence (which is really God's radical provision) has caused us to trust in our own abilities to get things done.

We are like the children of Israel whom God provided for at every turn. He parted a giant sea and dropped food from heaven to feed them, yet they still tried to control things. We wake up each day and hit the ground running for our own personal gain. We jump into the rat race with both feet, trying to control everything we can and tilt the world in our favor. We are taught to get an education, get a job, and grab as much money as we can while chasing the American dream. Society pressures us to fill our lives with things that make us happy or make us look successful. But is this the most God-honoring way to live? Does this lead to fulfillment and contentment or stress and anxiety? Let's examine this question further.

There is a combination of emptiness and stress in our culture today that is robbing many people of their joy. We are busier than ever but aren't even sure we are busy doing the right things. I'm afraid many people are going to reach the top of the ladder of success one day only to find out it was propped up against the wrong wall! There are many people who have acquired lots of stuff and achieved financial success yet remain unfulfilled. Our lack of fulfillment and contentment suggests we are in pursuit of many endeavors that have no eternal value or kingdom impact.

The apostle Paul said it best in Philippians 3:8, stating, "I consider everything a loss compared to the surpassing greatness of knowing Christ Jesus my Lord." In today's terms Paul's statement might look like this: I have achieved success at my job, but it's not as satisfying as knowing Jesus. I have built up my net worth, but it is not as fulfilling as being in the presence of the Lord. I have enjoyed many of life's pleasures, but nothing compares to the pleasure of knowing my eternity is secure. Paul knew the secret to contentment and fulfillment. What about us?

Our calendars are full, causing our anxiety (and blood pressure) to go through the roof. According to the Anxiety and Depression Association, over forty million adults suffer from anxiety disorders.[2] About seventy-five million American adults have high blood pressure.[3] I do realize this isn't all self-inflicted. The reality is our crazy-busy schedules are certainly not helping. So what is the answer? How can we slow down and find more meaning in life? The answer is we must relinquish control. We must resign from our self-appointed position as general manager of the universe.

The first chapter of Genesis tells us that Creator God is the maker of all things. If God is the maker of all things, then it should go without saying that he is also the owner of all things. When Apple invented the iPhone, they retained the rights of ownership. They didn't lose all their rights when others started

---

2 "About ADAA: Facts and Statistics," Anxiety and Depression Association of America, https://adaa.org/about-adaa/press-room/facts-statistics#.

3 Frumin, Aliyah. *America's silent killer is still out of control: Here's how to stop it.* (Today.com, October 18, 2017).

INTRODUCTION

using it. Psalm 50:10 tells us God owns the cattle on one thousand hills. I have news for you. He owns the hills as well. If he is the maker of all things and the owner of all things, then who is in control? God or us?

That is a fairly easy question to answer, which leads me to the primary topic of this book—surrender. Complete and total surrender to an almighty God. And stewardship. If we are going to surrender every area of our lives to God, we must recognize him as the owner. We are simply managers. Our time—given to us by him. Our talents—a gift from him. Our treasures—a blessing straight from God. Surrender becomes possible only when we give up ownership (and control) and become stewards. Managing his resources for his glory is the name of the game. If we can allow this truth to go from our heads to our hearts, everything changes. And our lives can again have meaning, purpose, and kingdom impact.

Scott Rodin, author of several great books on stewardship and surrender, had this to say about the steward's journey. "The journey of the faithful steward is the path of discipleship, obedience, discovery, adventure, service, and joy. It is the way of freedom and the way of the cross. It is the journey of every follower of Jesus. It is on this journey that we experience deeper levels of surrender, increased intimacy with Christ, clearer identity, more robust faith, and greater passion to serve. It is the path upon which we become the image-bearers of Christ in our world."[4]

If you are not a Christian or if you struggle with doubt, this message of surrender and stewardship may not make a lot of sense to you. However, I strongly encourage you to at least read chapters 12 and 13. They will give you a simple overview of what Christians believe and why we believe it. My prayer is that the Gospel message will be communicated to you in an easy-to-understand way

---

[4] Scott Rodin, *The Steward's Journey*. InterVarsity Press, 2010.

and stir in your heart a desire to learn more about the life-changing message of Jesus Christ.

But this book was written for believers. It was written for Christ-followers who are tired of rules and want a true relationship with the Lord. It was written for Christians who are ready to give up control and plug into a power far greater than their own. This book was written for believers who want to take their faith to the next level and find true victory in Jesus.

Several years ago I had a conversation with a guy who claimed to be a Christian. He said he believed in Jesus and knew he was going to heaven, so "that was enough for him." His point was that heaven can't be bad, so once he punched his ticket, anything else he received would be gravy. As expected, his life at that time revealed very little fruit of a relationship with the Lord. This conversation troubled me because I'm afraid this mindset is shared by many who profess to be Christ-followers. Salvation isn't fire insurance. It is the beginning of a spiritual journey that impacts every area of your life. It is a decision to lay down your own cares, desires, and selfish ways and surrender everything to the new Lord of your life. Salvation isn't the end goal. It's the starting point for living a life of purpose, hope, and kingdom impact.

Think with me for just one second. The Gospel is either true or it isn't. As C. S. Lewis said in his classic book *Mere Christianity*, Jesus is either the Lord, a liar, or a complete lunatic.[5] There is no middle ground. He either existed or he didn't. He either rose from the grave or he didn't. The Bible is either true or it isn't. So what are the implications of this? If we believe the Bible is the inerrant word of God and is completely true, then everything changes. If Jesus is who he says he is, the implications are mind-boggling! That means there is a place called heaven where Christ-followers

---

5 C. S. Lewis, *Mere Christianity* (New York, New York: Harper Collins, 2001), pp. 52-53.

INTRODUCTION

spend eternity. That also means there is a place called hell, a place of torment and suffering, where those who reject Christ spend eternity apart from God.

If Christianity is true, Jesus died for me and wants me to live for him. He has work for me to do every day and has an incredible mission for my life. There are certain things he wants from me and certain things he does not want me to do. He has plans for me and desires a personal relationship with me. Wow! As a follower of Jesus Christ, I don't know how this powerful truth of the Gospel doesn't send us all to our knees in holy surrender. Yes, heaven will be great. But God said his kingdom will come on earth as it is in heaven. Like young Jesus when he was lost at the temple, we too must "be about our Father's business." We must surrender everything to his lordship and seek to be good stewards of all he entrusts to us on this earth.

We will explore the relationship between surrender and stewardship in the first chapter, but I feel it is important to mention one thing now. When God first began stirring my heart about writing a book, stewardship was the first topic that came to mind. It is a topic that is near and dear to my heart. However, I wrestled with God for months about this because stewardship has almost become a dirty word in our churches today. It has now become synonymous with fundraising campaigns and the pastor's annual tithing message.

This saddens me. It saddens me for two reasons. First of all, stewardship is so much more than just how we manage our finances. While personal finance is a huge part of it, it is not the only thing. We will spend a lot of time discussing money, but we will also look at stewardship through this biblical lens: God owns it *all*, and I'm just the manager of what he entrusts to me. *All* is emphasized here because all means *all*. My money, my stuff, and even me. That's right. I am not even my own. I don't even own me. More on this later.

Surrendering to WIN

The second reason this saddens me is even if stewardship were all about money, we would still have the right to talk about it in church without criticism. Why do pastors have to tread lightly around the topic of money and possessions when Jesus spent a significant amount of time in his ministry discussing it? Jesus knew that money and possessions would be two of the chief competitors he would have for the thrones of our hearts. He also knew that our hearts and minds tend to drift in the same direction as our money.

If you do not believe this, consider what would happen if you were to take all your money and purchase a single stock. You would immediately become interested in that company's stock price, annual revenue, and spending decisions. Your ears would perk up when you heard them mentioned on the news, and you would likely read any article you saw about your new investment. For this reason, I think money should be preached about, taught, and openly discussed regularly. There are over twenty-three hundred verses in the Bible about money and possessions. It is rather obvious God wants us to win in this area of our lives.

Stewardship is a beautiful word. When used in its Christian context, it represents a high level of spiritual maturity. According to James Engel, who created the Engel Scale, it actually represents the highest level of maturity a Christian can obtain.[6] It should be embraced, not avoided, as we move forward on our spiritual journeys. We were given a stewardship assignment in the very beginning of time. After God created the earth, he created us to take care of it. The first responsibility given to mankind was to manage God's property well.

Surrender is a word that can be confused with weakness. In the Christian life, it is anything but that. Surrender actually

---

6 James Engel, *Munson Mission Musings: Multi–Dimensional Evangelism* (munsonmissions.org, November 13, 2010).

INTRODUCTION

represents power. Dying to self and tapping into God's power. Acknowledging a superior authority and submitting to his plan for your life. Praying and obeying. Surrendering to stewardship and surrendering to win. Jesus said whoever is least (last) in his kingdom will actually be first. Surrender and stewardship are very connected. They go hand in hand for the Christ-follower. Both require a great deal of humility. This book takes a strong look at this unique relationship.

In a "dog eat dog" world where we are encouraged to grab life by the tail and get our piece of the pie, why would we consider taking a back seat to what God wants to do in the world? What if his plan for us doesn't line up with what we want out of life? For the Christ-follower, this is a tough question that demands tough answers. Won't we get behind if we aren't aggressively pursuing our own goals? When we fully understand the Gospel and how we are commanded to respond to it, this question gets answered. Actually, the question stops getting asked. We surrender. We lay our lives and plans down at the feet of Holy God and beg him to take control of our life. We begin to view everything we have, including the very breath we breathe, as a gift from God. And the burning desire of our hearts becomes to honor God with the way we manage everything he entrusts to our care. We strive to make sure he gets the glory for anything that is accomplished in and through our lives.

That's where stewardship comes in. And that's what this book is all about. We will explore how to best manage our time, talents, and treasures. What does it look like to surrender our time to the Lord and steward it well? How can we use our unique giftedness (talents) for his kingdom? And how does surrender and stewardship apply to our money and possessions? The answers to these questions are critical to being all that God wants us to be and achieving victory in our spiritual lives.

In the final section, we will unpack the greatest act of surrender and greatest stewardship opportunity, which is the Gospel message of Jesus Christ. Surrendering our lives to the good news of Jesus Christ then stewarding this Gospel message well is a must. Our lives literally depend on us getting this right.

A critical component to daily surrender and biblical stewardship is prayer. Living a surrendered life is impossible without constant communication with our Creator. We must go to him early and often in our day. If we truly want to deny self and let him lead, a strong prayer life is vital. When we leave God out of our day, our natural tendencies are to insert ourselves into that gap.

Unfortunately, this does not work. We can't lead and expect God to follow. He isn't a genie in a bottle whom we call out when we need him. True surrender means every aspect of our lives is under the authority of Father God, and this begins and ends with prayer. James 5:16 tells us "the prayer of a righteous man is powerful and effective." Let me encourage you to stop right now and pray. Ask God to begin to change your heart. Ask him to reveal those areas of your life you are holding back from him. And ask him to help you let go of control and experience complete and total surrender.

One final word before we jump into the meat and potatoes. I am not a pastor. I am not even in full-time vocational ministry. I am certainly not a writer. I tell you this because I want you to know there is nothing special about Neal Broome. I am an ordinary guy who serves an extraordinary God. Chances are I am just like you. I am an American Christian who loves his family, works hard, and tries to do the next right thing. I am a basketball player who turned into a financial advisor. I have a selfishness that God remedied by allowing me to be a husband and a father. My competitive spirit makes daily surrender a real struggle for me. Therefore, I am really not worthy to teach you anything about this topic.

There are so many others who have gone before me and produced excellent material on surrender and stewardship. I have

INTRODUCTION

benefited greatly from the teachings of Dave Ramsey and Ron Blue in the areas of financial stewardship. Randy Alcorn, Scott Rodin, and many others have taken the topic of stewardship theology much deeper than I ever could take it. I am also grateful for pastor Andy Stanley of Northpoint Church in Atlanta and his teachings on stewarding time, money, and the gospel wisely. Because I stand on the shoulders of these great leaders, I do not feel worthy to place my name on this material.

So why write a book? This book is being written in simple obedience to what I believe God is calling me to do. I'm not worthy—he is. In my own strength, I do not have what it takes to pen these words. Thankfully, this book isn't dependent upon me. I have him. I wrestled with this for a few years because I knew how difficult writing a book would be. But God isn't interested in my excuses. So I surrendered. Yes, I finally did the very thing I am encouraging you to do through this book. That just shows I need this message as much as anyone. Probably more. Let's begin.

Simple Summary

At the end of each chapter, you will find a *simple summary*. The simple summary consists of five key points to remember from the content of the chapter. Each point is brief and designed to reinforce the core messages of the chapter.

Chapter 1

SURRENDERED STEWARDSHIP

Therefore, I urge you, brothers, in view of God's mercy, to offer your bodies as living sacrifices, holy and pleasing to God—this is your Spiritual act of worship.
—ROMANS 12:1

World War II was one of the most far-reaching and deadliest wars in the history of the world. It lasted six years (1939–1945) and involved over thirty different countries. It is estimated that seventy to eighty-five million people lost their lives in this brutal war. The effects of World War II were devastating and took many years to get past. Yet it could have been even worse. Something happened on August 15, 1945, that changed everything. Japan announced its intention to surrender. This one act all but sealed the deal for the Allies, bringing an end to the war. Japan recognized their weaknesses and knew an Allied invasion was imminent. So, after many years of fighting, they gave up.

Not everyone was in favor of Japan's surrender. There were many people, including some Japanese leaders, who wanted to continue fighting. They saw surrender as a cowardly act. Is that the case? It depends. Let's look at exactly what it means to surrender. As previously mentioned, it is usually seen as a sign of weakness. *Merriam-Webster* defines surrender as "giving up completely or agreeing to forgo one thing in favor of something else."[1] We don't like the sound of giving up. Our toughness and pride resist it. From a very early age, we are taught to never quit or give in. No one wants to be a quitter. No one wants to be viewed as weak. No one wants to surrender. Since winning is everything, surrender isn't an option.

But what if I told you that you were quitting something that wasn't working in favor of something that would work? What if this type of surrender actually traded your weakness for someone else's strength and made you a winner in the things that matter most? Such is the case with biblical surrender.

I am the proud father of young twin boys, Max and Miles. They love superheroes, Ninja Turtles, and anything that can fight and win. Sometimes they will ask me absurd questions like, "Daddy, can anyone jump over this house?" or "Is anyone strong enough to beat up a grizzly bear?" After I give them my usual answer of "No," their response is typically "God can! He can do everything!" Yes, he can! God can do anything he desires, even if it means jumping over houses and beating up bears.

That's the God to whom we need to surrender everything. When we discuss biblical surrender, we aren't talking about giving up on life or throwing in the towel on our responsibilities. Biblical surrender is an acknowledgment that we are weak but he is strong. We are helpless but he is all-powerful. We have a limited point of view but he holds the world in the palm of his hand. We serve a massive God, and when we recognize the magnitude of that incredible truth, surrender should be our natural response. He can be trusted, which is of utmost importance if we are going to embrace surrender. Even Jesus surrendered to Father God and said, "Yet not my will, but yours be done." True victory is only possible when we lay our feeble lives at the foot of the cross and hide ourselves in him.

---

1 Merriam-Webster.com, "Surrender."

SURRENDERED STEWARDSHIP

We are simply not capable of fully understanding the greatness of our God. He is *the* God who was and is and is to come. He is the beginning and the end. He exists outside of time. He spoke the world into existence. He can part seas, calm storms, heal the sick, and raise the dead. He is the Lion and the Lamb. He is the King of Kings and Lord of Lords. He is the Great I Am. His power and knowledge are without limits. He is omnipotent and omnipresent. He is sovereign over all things. He is our Savior and Provider. He is our Comforter and our Keeper. He is our Rock, and he is our Friend. He is our Helper in time of need. *He is God!*

In the book of Revelation, John has a vision of the throne room of God. John describes him as having head and hair white like wool, eyes like blazing fire, bronze feet glowing like a furnace, and a voice like the sound of rushing waters. He has a double-edged sword in his mouth, his face shines like the sun, and he holds stars in his hands. And that doesn't even begin to describe the beauty, glory, and majesty all around him! No wonder the angels all sing, "Holy, holy, holy is the Lord God Almighty!" Likewise, when our feet hit the floor each morning, we should fall to our knees and thank the good Lord above for allowing us another opportunity to enjoy another day. Are you starting to get the picture?

Maybe this will help you understand surrender. In the late eighties and early nineties, Iron Mike Tyson was in his prime. His climb to the top of the world boxing ranks was as fast as it was impressive. Michael Spinks lasted ninety-one seconds against the champ. Trevor Berbick went down for the count in round two. Tyson KO'd twelve of his first nineteen opponents in the first three minutes of the fight. Tyson's fierce approach, compact build, and iron-like punches were a recipe for disaster if you stood opposed to him.

So picture this: I am 6'7" and weigh 210 pounds on a good day (by good day I mean a day I've been to Krispy Kreme!). I've never boxed in my life. I also do not like confrontation, and I'm definitely not an aggressive person. So what would happen if I had to step into the ring against Iron Mike in his prime? Yes, you guessed it. Surrender. Complete and total surrender! Short of them telling me I get a million dollars if I stay on my feet a certain amount of time, I am going to lie down as soon as the bell sounds and help the referee count to ten. You get the picture. He is strong. I am not. He is powerful. I am not. He knows what he is doing. I do not. The best option I have is to raise the white flag. Actually, if I wanted to win, my best option would be to stop fighting and go stand in his corner!

Speaking of white flags, I love the words of Chris Tomlin's song from 2012. "We raise our white flag. We surrender. All to You. All for You. We raise our white flag: the war is over. Love has come, your love has won." Here is the most beautiful truth about this type of surrender: It is good. The battle has already been won. While most surrender is viewed as a negative, this is the ultimate positive. It requires sacrifice. It requires humility. It requires us to let go of control. But it is worth it! Not because of anything we can do, but because of what *he* can do in and through us when we surrender. As Pastor Rick Warren says, "Biblical surrender is the heart of worship." He goes on to say that "surrender is best demonstrated in obedience."[2]

So what does that have to do with stewardship? If surrender is defined as giving up and letting someone else have control, then how is it connected to being a good steward? Let's first examine stewardship and what exactly it means in a biblical context.

According to *Merriam-Webster*, stewardship can be defined as the careful and responsible management of something entrusted to one's care.[3] There are other definitions listed, but

---

2 Rick Warren, *The Purpose Driven Life* (Grand Rapids, Michigan: Zondervan, 2002).
3 Merriam-Webster.com, "Stewardship."

this one most closely describes the type of stewardship we are called to as followers of Jesus. A biblical worldview of stewardship requires us to manage all God's resources for his glory and for the betterment of his creation. John MacArthur once said, "All Christians are but God's stewards. Everything we have is on loan from the Lord, entrusted to us for a while to use in serving Him." If this feels heavy and overwhelming, be encouraged! While biblical stewardship is a great responsibility, it also presents us with a great opportunity!

Listen to these powerful and exciting words from Got (Bible) Questions Ministries: "The biblical doctrine of stewardship defines a man's relationship to God. It identifies God as owner and man as manager. God makes man His coworker in administering all aspects of our life." The apostle Paul explains it best by saying, "For we are God's fellow workers; you are God's field, God's building" (1 Cor. 3:9). Starting with this concept, we are then able to accurately view and correctly value not only our possessions but also, more importantly, human life itself. In essence, stewardship defines our purpose in this world as assigned to us by God himself. It is our divinely given opportunity to join with God in his worldwide and eternal redemptive movement (Matt. 28:19–20). Stewardship is not God taking something from us; it is his method of bestowing his richest gifts upon his people."[4]

In Matthew 25:14–30, Jesus tells a beautiful story about stewardship that has become known as the Parable of the Talents.

> Again, it will be like a man going on a journey, who called his servants and entrusted his wealth to them. To one he gave five bags of gold, to another two bags, and to another one bag, each according to his ability. Then he went on

---

[4] Got Questions Ministries. "What is Biblical Stewardship?" (gotquestions.org, January 2, 2020).

his journey. The man who had received five bags of gold went at once and put his money to work and gained five bags more. So also, the one with two bags of gold gained two more. But the man who had received one bag went off, dug a hole in the ground and hid his master's money.

After a long time, the master of those servants returned and settled accounts with them. The man who had received five bags of gold brought the other five. "Master," he said, "you entrusted me with five bags of gold. See, I have gained five more."

His master replied, "Well done, good and faithful servant! You have been faithful with a few things; I will put you in charge of many things. Come and share your master's happiness!"

The man with two bags of gold also came. "Master," he said, "you entrusted me with two bags of gold; see, I have gained two more."

His master replied, "Well done, good and faithful servant! You have been faithful with a few things; I will put you in charge of many things. Come and share your master's happiness!"

Then the man who had received one bag of gold came. "Master," he said, "I knew that you are a hard man, harvesting where you have not sown and gathering where you have not scattered seed. So I was afraid and went out and hid your gold in the ground. See, here is what belongs to you."

His master replied, "You wicked, lazy servant! So you knew that I harvest where I have not sown and gather where I have not scattered seed? Well then, you should have put my money on deposit with the bankers, so that when I returned, I would have received it back with interest.

So take the bag of gold from him and give it to the one who has ten bags. For whoever has will be given more, and they will have an abundance. Whoever does not have, even what they have will be taken from them. And throw that worthless servant outside, into the darkness, where there will be weeping and gnashing of teeth."

In this parable there are some things made very clear about stewardship:

1) A proper view of ownership must be established. It is clear that the master is the rightful owner and the servants are simply being trusted with the master's resources.
2) Accountability and expectations play a part when we are managing property that isn't our own. We cannot simply do what we want to do or whatever feels best. We must manage what is entrusted to us according to the rightful owner's plan.
3) There are rewards for a job well done. When we are trustworthy and faithful in our assignment, we get an "attaboy" from the owner. And in many cases, our responsibilities increase (more on this later).

Here is a question you can ask yourself to see how you are doing in the area of stewardship: Am I using what has been entrusted to me to build my own kingdom or God's kingdom? If we are honest in our answers, there is a good chance we must say we've gotten off track in the management of God's resources.

I mentioned in the introduction that James Engel has charted the levels of spiritual maturity. Below is his chart representing the journey of faith for a person who begins with no knowledge of God and ultimately achieves a high level of spiritual maturity:

Surrendering to WIN

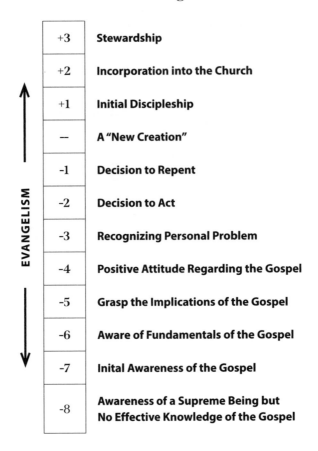

So why would someone view stewardship in such high regard? Because biblical stewardship puts an almighty God high and exalted on his throne, where he belongs, and puts insignificant us at his feet, where we belong. It is the way it was originally designed. After God created the earth, he placed man in the garden to work it and care for it. Fast-forward thousands of years, and we have attempted to take over ownership of the garden and place God in it to work for us. It just doesn't work that way. Herein lies the connection between stewardship and surrender. When our view of our Heavenly Father is that of an all-powerful, all-knowing Creator of the universe, acknowledging him as owner of all things just makes sense. And surrender becomes our

SURRENDERED STEWARDSHIP

natural response. If he is Creator, he is in control, not me. This truth commands surrender.

I asked my pastor to share his thoughts on the connection between biblical surrender and biblical stewardship. This was his response:

> "I have grown in my understanding of stewardship through the years. Stewardship is more than giving—it is more than tithing—the 10 percent. Biblical stewardship involves how we use 100 percent of what He has given us. There have been times in my life when I used the tithe as a finish line—if I've tithed, then I thought I had done my part. Other times I have felt good that I freely gave above the tithe, but I'm afraid I thought I had done my part then, too, and did not consider God's ownership of all that I have.
>
> If Jesus is Lord of my life, then everything I have is his: my money, my time, my gifts, my family, and my opportunities. Stewardship is more than giving; it is more than money. Stewardship involves all my life. I love the hymn "I Surrender All," but I must confess there are times I struggle to live out the lyrics of the first verse:
>
> All to Jesus I surrender;
> All to Him I freely give.
> I will ever love and trust Him,
> In His presence daily live.
>
> God has been totally faithful to me and has blessed me in ways I do not deserve. I have always had enough, and I can say I have always had more than enough. I owe God thanks for every blessing in my life. I should be willing to surrender everything to him because he surrendered his life for me."

I could not agree more! So what does this look like lived out in a very practical way? We will spend the rest of this book unpacking the answer to that question. But for summary's sake, here is an overview of practical surrender and practical stewardship. Surrendering every area of our lives to God requires us to let go of control. It requires us to trust daily in God's promises and in his provision. It is an acceptance that he has a plan, and that it is a plan for our good. Biblical surrender decreases worry and increases faith. It allows us to weather life's storms because we know that God can work all things together for good.

We will all eventually surrender our lives to something or someone. Whether it's your money, your job, your family, or something else, there are many things that compete for first place in our lives. Only God is worthy of our complete and total surrender. Stewardship acknowledges God's ownership of everything. Literally everything. All that we have and all that we are is from God. When our hearts are aligned with this biblical truth, we seek to manage every aspect of our life his way and for his glory. Stewardship isn't just about money. It's a lifestyle. It's a worldview in and of itself. And it's the correct worldview. Remember, total surrender and biblical stewardship starts with prayer. Falling on our knees before a holy God aligns our hearts with what he has for our life.

The enemy of surrender and stewardship is Satan. He uses our pride and fears against us. Just like he did with Adam and Eve, he constantly encourages us to do things our way and blaze our own trail. He wants nothing more than to recruit an army of selfish, greedy control freaks who couldn't care less about God. If he can keep us focused on and worshipping the creation and not the Creator, he wins. In 1 Peter 5:8, Peter tells us the devil prowls around like a roaring lion looking for someone to devour. We must resist the devil if we are going to live the surrendered life. James 4:7 says, "Submit yourselves then to God. Resist the devil and he will flee from you."

We must equip ourselves with the armor of God if we are going to be good managers of the Lord's resources. Pastor Tony

SURRENDERED STEWARDSHIP

Evans says that when our feet hit the floor each morning, the devil and his army should cry out, "Oh no! They're awake!" The only way to win this battle is to walk daily in the power of the word and the Holy Spirit. We cannot do this alone. We must relinquish control to almighty God. Victory becomes possible when we are fully surrendered to him.

I love the game of basketball. I started playing when I was really young and still try to play a few times each week. When I was a senior in high school, I led the state of Mississippi in scoring, averaging thirty-three points per game. But that same season also produced one of the low moments of my playing career. We were locked in a tight battle with one of our district rivals. As the clock ticked down with my team trailing by one point, I heaved a half-court shot to try to win the game. The shot missed badly, but the referees called a foul, sending me to the line to shoot three free throws.

With no time showing on the clock and the home team leading by one point, an 84 percent free throw shooter walked to the line with a chance to claim victory. All I needed to do was make two out of three. As I stepped to the free throw line, I noticed something happening I had never seen before. The other team began heading to their locker room. They surrendered. In their minds the game was over, and they had lost. I made the first free throw to tie the game. Now some of their fans headed for the exits. At this point nearly everyone on the home side had given up. Our fans, on the other hand, were standing up proclaiming victory. Then I missed. Then I missed again. Then we lost in overtime.

Humans will let you down. I let my team and our fans down that day. God will never fail you. He is the same yesterday, today, and forever. When we fully surrender to him, he leads us to victory. God doesn't miss free throws. He doesn't make mistakes. He cannot lie, and he cannot let us down. Thankfully, our salvation and spiritual maturity isn't dependent upon our own efforts. (I am also thankful those things aren't dependent upon our ability to make free throws!) It is not about us. It is all about God.

In a world where we are encouraged to be selfish and take control, following his commands is not easy. Biblical stewardship takes discipline and maturity and requires complete surrender. Most of the time, we do not surrender and are not good stewards because we like to be in control. In the next chapter, we will unpack this unhealthy desire most of us wrestle with daily.

Simple Summary

1) Biblical surrender means letting God have control over every area of your life.
2) By surrendering we actually become stronger because of God's power.
3) Stewardship acknowledges God's ownership of all his creation. We are simply managers of what he entrusts to us.
4) Biblical stewardship represents a high level of spiritual maturity.
5) Satan does all he can to lead us away from complete surrender and good stewardship.

Chapter 2

CONTROL FREAKS

*Jesus looked at them and said,
"With man this is impossible,
but with God all things are possible."*
—Matthew 19:26

We live in a Burger King world in which we want everything our way right away. The second part of their slogan speaks to a completely different issue—our impatience. I'm not going to focus on our desire to have things "right away." This chapter is about our desire to do things "our way." Let's face it. Most of us are control freaks. Letting go of control goes against our very nature. We believe if something is going to get done, we should lead the charge to make it happen. Our inability to let go causes stress, anxiety, and other health issues. Yet we continue because the alternative is to not have a direct say in final outcomes. So day after day, we wake up and act as though it depends on us to keep the earth in orbit. We find it very hard to say no to anything, and we do it in the name of "It's part of my job" or "I need to make sure it's done correctly." Let me stop here and say that this mentality often leads to success. A hard-charging, "take the bull by the horns" attitude can lead to great outcomes. But it can also wear you out completely. And it can cause us to miss what God is trying to do in us and through us.

Surrendering to WIN

One of my favorite life quotes is "Paddle the boat and pray for wind." If you are a professional sailor, please forgive me if I "miss the boat" on this next illustration. Picture yourself in a small sailboat in the middle of a large body of water. Your ability to move where you want to go is controlled by the two paddles that came with the boat and the small sail that extends off the bow. If your desire is to move to the northeast corner of the lake, what should you do? The obvious answer is to pick up the two paddles and begin paddling in the desired direction. But there is a second element in play here. The sail on the boat needs wind behind it to move the vessel in a particular direction. Do we control the wind? No. Can we adjust the sail so the wind takes us in the direction we want to go? Yes. But here is the key point: No matter how hard we paddle, the wind has the ability to limit our movement and even cause us to go in a different direction. Such is the case in our lives. There is work for us to do every day. But God's plan will prevail. It is our job to do everything we can to live according to his word and then adjust our sails to move in the direction in which he wants us to go. Let me illustrate this another way.

Giving up control doesn't mean sitting around doing nothing and waiting on the Lord to provide for our every need. Biblical surrender doesn't mean becoming passive or lazy. Let's say you lose your job tomorrow. The "control freak" would obsessively hammer out thirteen versions of his resume, knock on every door within a fifty-mile radius, and be stressed to the max when he didn't have a job offer in thirty-six hours. This is a "paddle hard and don't pray" approach. The passive "I'm just going to trust God" guy would sleep in every day for six months, catch up on all his TV shows, and wonder, after six months, why God had not provided gainful employment. This is a "no paddle, all prayer" (maybe!) approach. The right approach is to do your due diligence in seeking employment you feel fits your God-given design and allows you to use your strengths while praying daily for him to open some doors and close others. It is a balance between doing our part and relying on him to work out his plan in his perfect timing. God cannot steer a parked car. We must be moving if we want him to guide us.

There are several examples from scripture that show us this balance in action. In Exodus 17, the Israelite army found themselves engaged in a heated battle with the Amalekites. Moses, their leader, had just spent time with the Lord to address another issue: the children of Israel were thirsty and had no water. God told Moses to use his staff to strike a rock and that water would come out. Moses was obedient and did his part. When he struck the rock, God provided. Now, in the heat of battle, Moses had a different role to play. This same staff had to be held up to God in order for the Israelite army to win the battle. As long as Moses was holding up the staff and doing his part, they were winning. Whenever he lowered his hands, the Amalekites took control. Ultimately, the Israelites prevailed. Moses did his part, and God did the rest.

Joshua became the new Israelite leader when Moses passed away. He found himself in a "paddle and pray" scenario in Joshua 6. When he consulted the Lord as to how to overcome this powerful city, the Lord's response was "march around the city once with all the armed men. Do this for six days. Have seven priests carry trumpets of rams' horns in front of the ark. On the seventh day, march around the city seven times with the priests blowing the trumpets. When you hear them sound a long blast on the trumpets, have all the people give a loud shout. Then the wall of the city will collapse, and the people will go up, every man straight in" (Josh. 6:3–5).

So what did Joshua do? Exactly what God told him to do! The next few verses show his perfect obedience to the task he was given. And what did God do? He honored Joshua's obedience and collapsed the wall, allowing the Israelite army to take the city.

Surrendering to WIN

In obedience Joshua "paddled" as hard as he could around and around that massive wall. Some folks probably thought he was crazy. Maybe they even made fun of such a great leader giving such a silly command. But Joshua trusted God. He surrendered to the simple instructions God had given him. And I'm sure Joshua prayed. He was committed to doing his part and trusting God to do the rest. It's a beautiful formula. And it works. And it leads to peace. And victory!

I think it is fair to say we sometimes overcomplicate things. We are wired for adventure, excitement, and big deals. Faithful stewardship and total surrender apply to the smallest of the small just as much as to the biggest of the big in our lives. Jesus tells us this in one of his parables about a shrewd manager (Luke 16:10). We must be faithful in the little things if we want to be trusted with bigger things. Every detail matters to God.

In 2 Kings 5, we read about a commander of the king's army named Naaman. Naaman was a great man and a highly regarded soldier, but he had leprosy. At the suggestion of a young girl, he sets out on a journey to visit Elisha with the hope of being cured of his leprosy. Elisha's instructions to Naaman were quite simple: go wash in the Jordan River seven times and you will be healed. This was not what Naaman wanted to hear! He stormed away, angry at the simplicity of Elisha's message. Naaman was expecting fireworks and some big show. Instead he got a simple task from God's prophet. After he got over his initial disgust, Naaman humbled himself and went to the river. He surrendered and obeyed. After doing his part and dipping himself into the river seven times, God did his part and cured Naaman of his leprosy. On that day Naaman became a believer in the God of Israel.

Make no mistake about it: God can do whatever he wants whenever he wants. He doesn't need us to accomplish anything. Consider the invalid in John 5 who was hanging out near the pool of Bethesda. He had been in this condition for thirty-eight years. Jesus could have easily asked this man to do something that would lead to healing. Instead, he said to him in verse 8, "Get up! Pick up your mat and walk." And verse 9 tells us "the man was cured. He picked up his mat and walked." God doesn't have to rely on us to accomplish his kingdom purposes. But he wants to use us. And that is a profound truth! He actually wants us to play a role in what he is doing in the world. God is in control, but we are his ambassadors. To stay in the center of his will, we must be obedient to the things he asks or commands us to do.

It is time we step down, step back, and let God be God. It's the oldest temptation in the book. We want to play God. Or, as in Adam and Eve's case, we want to be like God. This was the very reason Satan was thrown out of heaven. He wanted to be "the man." I have some bad news and some good news to share with you. Let's start with the bad news. We are not in control. No matter how hard we try and how much we think outcomes depend on us, the end result isn't in our hands. If you think about it, that's actually not bad news at all. It should be comforting news to hear. It should bring instant relief from our stressed-out, overloaded minds.

Now for the good news. Creator God *is* in control. Always has been, always will be. Period. End of discussion. That's not just good news. That's great news! Have you ever watched the movie *Bruce Almighty* starring Jim Carrey? He is granted a wish to become God and uses it to his advantage every chance he gets. Things really spiral out of control when Bruce is trying to answer the prayers of everyone on earth. He quickly realizes how complex the world is and that trying to make it all fit together is virtually impossible. Bruce can't handle it. God can. And he will. So let's give God the glory for each victory he accomplishes in and through us.

Why do we think we are so important to the success of the world? If you recall the creation story in Genesis, God created a lot of things before he even got around to us. As a matter of fact, we barely even found our way into the story. Right before he decided to take a break and rest, he made man. On the sixth day. Out of seven. This shows that he didn't need us around from day one telling him how to do things.

Another way to look at it is by examining the brevity of life. God always has been and always will be. He is Alpha and Omega, the beginning and the end. I was born in 1978 and will be gone by 2078 (probably a lot sooner!). By the way, "1978" represents the number of years that have passed since Jesus died. There are also several thousand years of biblical history recorded before that. My point is that people come and people go. The years fly by, and God's story continues to unfold. We simply have the great privilege of being able to participate in his great plan while we are here.

Again, it's his plan and not ours. He is responsible for working all things together for good, not us. If these thoughts leave you feeling unimportant, don't let them. This is the cool part. Yes, scripture tells us our lives on this earth are like a mist that is here today and gone tomorrow. And yes, God started this whole thing with no input or assistance from us. But he *did* create us, and he desires to use us to fulfill his mission. This unique relationship with him gives our lives incredible purpose. Our job is simple. Obedience and surrender. Getting out of God's way and allowing his plans to prosper. Humbly seeking what role we might play in his great story. He has given us the owner's manual, so we know what he wants us to do (and not do). This is where obedience comes in.

Author and speaker Lysa TerKeurst said it best when she said, "Our job is obedience. His job is everything else." When we live a surrendered life and allow God to work in and through us, everything changes. When we are obedient to his word and his call on our life, God leads us to the desired life he has for us. It's simple. But because we are human, it can be quite difficult.

The best way I've found to combat our fleshly desire to be in control is summed up in 1 Corinthians 6:19–20. "Do you not know your body is a temple of the Holy Spirit, who is in you, whom you have received from God? You are not your own. You were bought at a price. Therefore, honor God with your body." Talk about stewardship! This profound truth gets to the very heart of the owner/manager struggle. I don't even belong to me! Jesus purchased me when he died on the cross for my sins. I belong to him. When I gave my life to Christ and accepted his saving grace, I became his. I no longer get to do what Neal wants to do. I no longer call the shots. My life is now led by the Holy Spirit who lives in me. I have been crucified with Christ. I no longer live, but rather Christ now lives in me. If he says I am to do something, I need to do it.

That's where obedience comes in. If my agenda conflicts with his agenda, I must submit to his plan. That's where surrender comes in. As simple as this sounds, this is why it is a real challenge: Obedience and surrender are not one-time decisions. We must die to self every single day. Sometimes multiple times per day. Because we live in a broken world, new challenges present themselves at every turn. The enemy wants to derail our lives and keep us from being kingdom players. As we strive to live a Jesus-centered life, temptations and trials are sure to come. We must stay focused on the eternal and not get distracted by those things that threaten our witness. At the risk of sounding like I have this all figured out, I want to share with you one practical way I've equipped myself for the daily battle.

For several years I would stop at the end of my driveway before leaving for work and pray this (or a similar) prayer: "God, thank you for another day to go out and make a difference for You. Use me today however You desire to impact people for Your Kingdom. I surrender this day to You. I don't know what's in store for me, but You do. Fill me with Your Spirit and allow me to be a blessing to those You put in my path. My time and talents are a gift from You. Help me to use them to make a difference today. I love You. Amen." God honored this prayer time and time again. When my day started spiraling out of control, I could always feel his presence reminding me he was in control.

As life got more and more hectic and as my responsibilities grew, I felt like I needed more time with him to start my day. I contacted a local church and asked if they had a room I could visit each morning to spend time alone with God. The campus pastor was gracious enough to show me their prayer room and allow me to use it anytime. This quiet, spirit-filled room has become my war room. I stop by each day and equip myself for battle. My prayers have not changed. However, I've added quality time in the word to my arsenal.

Satan has no chance. Not because of me. In my own strength, I would fail miserably. But I have embraced the fact that I am not my own. I belong to Jesus. I surrender each day to him. I lean on him to fight my battles. I trust him to lead and guide my decisions. I'm not perfect. But I serve a God who is! I serve a God who has unlimited power (omnipotence), knows everything (omniscience), and is everywhere (omnipresent). Allow these truths to go from your head to your heart, and surrender becomes much easier.

We should be radically surrendered Jesus freaks. Instead we journey on, looking much more like control freaks. Actually, when it comes to how we spend our time, we look much more like out-of-control freaks! We have overloaded our schedules with too many things that have no eternal value. Our time on this earth is a gift from God. We are just pilgrims passing through a strange land on our way to our heavenly home. We are living on borrowed time. Managing our time well is a must if we are going to be all God wants us to be. Let's examine this stewardship opportunity further.

CONTROL FREAKS

Simple Summary

1) We love to be in control.

2) We should work as if it depends on us but pray as if it depends on God. Paddle the boat, and pray for wind!

3) We need to resign as general managers of the universe.

4) When we surrender our lives to Christ, we are giving up control of outcomes to him.

5) Because God is all-powerful and all-knowing, we can trust him with our lives.

Section 1:
Our Time

Chapter 3

LIFE IS SHORT

Why, you do not even know what will happen tomorrow. What is your life? You are a mist that appears for a little while and then vanishes.

—James 4:14

A few years back, Reebok popularized the slogan "Life is short. Play hard." T-shirts were sold to thousands of athletes with these words printed on the front. Shortly thereafter a Christian print company made a slight change to the wording and began selling their own version. This time the shirt read, "Life is short. Pray hard." As a former athlete, I can appreciate the value of playing hard each time you compete. As a Christian, I am also fully supportive of the second slogan. Prayer is a vital part of your spiritual walk. But the focus of this chapter isn't playing or praying. The purpose of this chapter is to remind us of the brevity of life.

Again, the book of James compares our life to a mist that is here today and gone tomorrow. As a friend of mine often says, "The days are long, but the years are short." Time just seems to fly by! When I talk to people who are older than me, almost without fail they mention how they don't know where the years have gone. Senior adults speak of "the good old days" as though they were yesterday. We are so busy trying to meet all of life's demands, we hardly have time to slow down and enjoy anything. This leads me to a sobering reality: we only have a precious few years to make our lives count for something. The shortness of our time on this earth magnifies the need to surrender our lives to God.

My grandfather passed away when I was a young boy. Papa Mike was in his sixties when lung cancer claimed his life. While I only have a few vague memories of our time together, I still remember one thing very clearly—Mike King's funeral service. It was the first funeral I ever attended, so I struggled to understand what was taking place. In that memorial service, the congregation sang a song titled "What Will I Leave Behind?"

> After I leave for worlds unknown, over the borderline. Never again on Earth to roam. What will I leave behind?
>
> Will I be missed by those I love? Or have I been unkind? Have I been true to God above? What will I leave behind?
>
> This is my prayer dear Lord each day. Let me be holy thine. When I am called from Earth away. Let Heaven then be mine![1]

What will you leave behind? That is a great question to meditate on as you consider the brevity of life. At the risk of sounding morbid, let me just put this out there: we all have an appointment someday with death. One hundred percent of people who are born into this world will someday pass away. It doesn't matter if you are a Democrat or Republican. One day you will die. It doesn't matter if you are black or white. One day you will die. It doesn't matter if you are male or female. One day you will die. We don't like to think about death, but that doesn't change the reality of it. Each day that passes brings us closer to the end.

Are you ready for that day? Do you know where you would

---

[1] Sherrill Brown, "What Will I Leave Behind," 1958 (Renewed 1986, Stamps Quartet Music).

LIFE IS SHORT

spend eternity? Do you have your affairs in order? Are you prioritizing the relationships that God has entrusted to you? I know it's not fun to think about the shortness of life. We must, however, think ahead and be ready. A great question to ponder is: "If I knew my life was coming to an end in twelve months, what are some things I would immediately start (or stop) doing?"

I strongly encourage you to spend some time preparing for when that time comes. The most important thing you can do is to make sure you are saved. The next step is to get organized. In my home I have a fireproof safe that contains the following documents:

- My will and estate-planning documents
- Life insurance policies
- All recent bank statements
- Statements for investment accounts
- Funeral plans
- Legacy letters—these are letters to my wife, sons, church, family, and friends that I want read after I die
- My personal testimony—this is a one-page letter telling the story of when I surrendered my life to Jesus

On your tombstone will be a couple of numbers. The first number represents your arrival on planet earth. You have no control over this number. The second number will represent the time you depart from this world. Again, you have limited control over that number. In the middle, however, is a dash. The dash is usually very small but is a powerful character in your life story. What are you doing with your dash? Are you spending your precious moments on earth focused on the things that matter most? How you spend your dash is the one thing you have some control over. What you do with your dash will in large part determine the legacy you leave behind.

If you feel the weight of those last few words bearing down

on your shoulders, I have some good news for you. We don't live out our dash all at once. Nope. We live our lives one day at a time, one minute at a time, one breath at a time, one decision at a time. Think for a second about the old joke about eating an elephant. You would have to be really hungry to eat an entire elephant. But if you were tasked with this gigantic assignment, how would you accomplish it? The only way humanly possible. One bite at a time. If you woke up every day and ate one bite at a time for a certain period, eventually the entire elephant would be gone. The journey of one thousand miles begins with the first step. In the business world, this is known as the compound effect. Simply stated, consistent, positive daily actions multiplied by time gives you compounded results!

Exercise is the best example of this effect in action. If you wake up tomorrow and start a new exercise program, chances are you will be tired and sore the next day. If you allow this fatigue to discourage you from continuing the program, you will have wasted that workout. Working out again two months from now doesn't build on today's workout. If, however, you continued the workout day after day regularly, positive changes would start to happen. You would get past the soreness. Your muscles would begin to grow. You would likely lose weight. Your lungs would be able to handle more and more intensity. And your results would grow exponentially! So what does this have to do with surrender and spiritual growth?

Once we realize how short life is and how little time we have to make a difference here on this earth, our priorities should change. According to Statista, the average life expectancy in the United States for a female is eighty-one years; for a male, it's just seventy-six years.[2] We should treasure every day as the gift from God that it is. I once read, "Life is short, but it is up to you to make it

---

[2] Erin Duffin, *Statista.com/Society/Demographic*, September 20, 2019.

sweet." Our heart's desire should be to make every moment count.

As we begin to live with this type of focus and intentionality, our spiritual impact compounds. Daily surrender to God's word leads to spiritual growth and biblical wisdom. Daily time alone with God in prayer strengthens our relationship with him and helps us know him better. Daily commitment to obedience leads us into the plan God has for us.

It sounds simple, but it's these small daily steps that allow us to leap forward in our faith. Think for a second about the previous exercise example. This time let's substitute reading the Bible for exercising. If I wake up tomorrow and read two chapters of the Bible then head off to work, we would all likely agree this is a good thing. But if I then do not pick up my Bible the rest of this year, chances are there will not be any fruit in my life from my time in God's word. It's not that God can't use those few minutes I spend with him to speak to me. He can and likely will. But to keep moving forward in my faith journey, I must surrender to him day in, day out. Life is short. It is imperative we make every single day count.

There is an old Gospel hymn that used to be one of my favorites. The title is "One Day at a Time." Here is the chorus:

> One day at a time, sweet Jesus.
> That's all I'm asking from you.
> Just give me the strength to do every day what I have to do.
> Yesterday's gone, sweet Jesus.
> And tomorrow may never be mine.
> Lord, help me today, show me the way, one day at a time.[3]

I love the words of that song. It is a great reminder that yesterday is over, and we are not promised tomorrow. Today is the day that matters. This is the day the Lord has made. We are to

---

[3] Kris Kristofferson and Marijohn Wilkin, "One Day at a Time," 1974 (Singer: Marilyn Sellars).

rejoice and be glad in it. Many times we ruin our todays because we live with guilt from yesterday and worries about tomorrow. Jesus spoke very clearly about this when he said in Matthew 6:34, "Do not worry about tomorrow, for tomorrow will worry about itself. Each day has enough trouble of its own."

Listen, friends. Yesterday is history, and tomorrow is a mystery, but today is a present. Embrace today. Surrender it to God. Esther knew the importance of one day. Everything that had happened to her seemed to culminate in one moment of decision. One opportunity to make a difference. Her one shining moment would come after Haman had tricked King Xerxes into signing a decree to kill all Jews. Esther had gone from a poor nobody to a favored queen in a short amount of time, but now her people were in danger. She was in danger. And she was really the only hope they had of surviving. She was being asked to go to the king and plead with him. However, if she were to come before the king without being summoned, she could be put to death.

Hear the words of Mordecai to Esther in Esther 4:13–14. "He sent back this answer: do not think that because you are in the king's house, you alone of all the Jews will escape [interpreted—don't forget you too are a Jew and will also die]. For if you remain silent at this time, relief and deliverance for the Jews will arise from another place, but you and your father's family will perish. And who knows but that you have come to your royal position for such a time as this." If ever there was a God-ordained moment, this was it.

You probably know the rest of the story. The king honors all Esther's requests, the Jews are spared, and Haman ends up being impaled by the very pole he had set up for the Jews. God is good! And his plans will always prevail. Is there something big God is wanting to do in your life today? Just surrender. Day by day, moment by moment, decision by decision. Surrender it all to him. *Surrender to win.*

Most people have greater regrets about the things in life they

LIFE IS SHORT

didn't do than the things they did do. Embrace each day! Take advantage of every God-ordained opportunity he puts in front of you. If he is for you, who can be against you? Imagine what would have happened if Andrew, Peter, James, and John had handled Jesus's request to follow him the way we do. We tend to over-analyze, procrastinate, and drag our feet before we get moving. The Bible tells us that these men *immediately* put down what they were doing and pursued Jesus.

Let's return to our dash. If we want our dash to have a lasting impact on people, we must establish good habits. We will discuss this in more detail in the next chapter, but here is a fascinating fact to consider. According to a recent Duke University study, 40 percent of the decisions we make every day are a result of pre-programmed habits.[4] Simply put, we are creatures of habit. We love (and even crave) routine. This makes doing the right things and avoiding the wrong things critically important. Especially if we desire to leave a positive legacy and, more importantly, make a kingdom impact with our life. Ralph Waldo Emerson said that when you sow a thought, you reap an action; sow an action, reap a habit; sow a habit, reap a character; sow a character, reap a destiny. Since kingdom impact begins with our thought-life, we must guard our minds and take every thought captive. Victory in our minds leads to victory in our actions.

I mentioned at the start of this chapter some popular slogans about the brevity of life. One I failed to mention is this: "Life is short, and then you die." While it is true, these words paint a negative picture that leaves out something beautiful that God designed. Yes, life is short, but eternity is forever! That's right. Our time on this troubled earth isn't all there is to look forward to. If we live fifty, sixty, seventy, or even eighty years, that time

---

[4] Duhigg, Charles. *The Power of Habit* (New York: Random House Publishing, 2014).

pales in comparison to our time in eternity. Eternity is, well, eternal. Never-ending. Forever and ever. For followers of Jesus, time doesn't matter on the other side of death. We will spend eternity in heaven with our Lord and Savior Jesus Christ. Like the old hymn says: ten thousand years and we have just begun.

There are not many things that make me happier than this thought. When my short life here ends, I am going to a place of perfect peace, perfect love, and perfect rest. I will spend eternity worshipping the King of Kings and the Lord of Lords. I will be reunited with loved ones who have gone on before me. There will be no fighting, arguing, or death. There will be no pain, suffering, or disease. Everything will be perfect. Every wrong will be made right. And the best news is, this will never end! I will sit at the feet of Jesus in awe and utter amazement and worship him throughout eternity.

So, while my time here may be limited, I'm ok with that. My focus is on that which isn't limited. My hope is in a place where my body will not move closer to deterioration with every breath I take. What drives me here on this earth isn't the seventy-five to eighty years I will spend here. It's the promise of the ten thousand–plus after that.

Randy Alcorn uses a dot and a line to illustrate this point. If you were to take a pen and draw a tiny dot at the very corner of a piece of paper then extend a line out from the dot that goes all the way across the page, this could help us understand this life versus the eternal. The dot represents our time here. The line (which never ends) represents eternity.[5] Why in the world do we obsess so much about "dot decisions?" Many of the things we concern ourselves with each day have no eternal value. Our focus should be on the line. The Bible tells us that God put eternity in our hearts. We need to lift our eyes above the chaos of our current

---

5 Randy Alcorn. *Treasure Principle* (Colorado Springs, Colorado: Multnomah Books, 2001).

LIFE IS SHORT

world and lock in on that which is eternal. Therein lies the secret to making each day count.

Psalm 90:12 says, "Teach us to number our days that we may gain a heart of wisdom." This psalm, most likely written by Moses, could very well be the oldest psalm. The commentary from my NIV Study Bible says it this way, "Realizing that life is short helps us use the little time we have more wisely and for eternal good. Take time to number your days by asking, 'What do I want to see happen in my life before I die? What small step could I take toward that purpose today?'"

In the verses leading up to verse 12, Moses tells us: 1) God is eternal and not limited by time; 2) life is short and full of trouble; and 3) God is powerful, and only through him can our lives have meaning. Then we come to verse 12. Moses is literally crying out to God and saying, "God help me to live as though my days are numbered. Help me realize that my time on Earth is short and limited. Since my days are limited, help me make wise decisions." This next chapter discusses wise decisions and the consequences of poor decisions.

Simple Summary

1) Our time on this earth is very limited.

2) Every day is a gift from God and an opportunity to participate in his kingdom work.

3) Eternity is forever. Ten thousand years will only be the beginning of our time in heaven (or hell).

4) We need to focus on the eternal and not the temporal.

5) What are you doing with your dash?

Chapter 4

CHOICES AND CONSEQUENCES

Do not be deceived: God cannot be mocked.
A man reaps what he sows.
—Galatians 6:7

About three doors down from the gym where I work out, there is a bakery. Each morning people park their cars in a shared parking lot. Some walk in the gym. Others go get a donut. One day, while on the treadmill, I saw an elderly man get out of his truck in gym clothes. As he was walking toward the gym door, he suddenly stopped dead in his tracks. He briefly paused, turned around, and began walking the other way. A few minutes later, he emerged from the bakery with a bag of goodies. He never set foot in the gym. I smiled as I thought about what had just taken place. Life is full of tough choices. And many of them are more important than deciding between the gym and a hot glazed donut. (Side note: if I live to be as old as that gentleman, I will likely choose the bakery too!)

I was once told that who a man eventually becomes is a result of the company he keeps and the books he reads. There is a lot of truth in this old saying. The things we allow into our minds and the people we allow into our sphere of influence certainly impact our attitudes and actions. I've always felt that if this is true, I am going to be ok. After all, I enjoy reading books that teach and encourage me, and I've always surrounded myself with pretty good people.

However, one day after sharing this with an older gentleman, he said to me, "Neal, that is only partially true. To take it one step further, I would propose who a man becomes is really more about the choices he makes and the consequences of his choices." Uh oh! With this one nugget of wisdom, my success plan was blown to bits. Reading a good book is a decision we make. The consequence of that decision is usually that we learn something or are inspired in some way. Hanging out with good people is a decision we make. The result of this decision is we are influenced in a positive manner. He took my philosophy and expanded it. And his statement has proven to be true over and over again. Good decisions lead to desired outcomes. Bad decisions lead to negative consequences. We've all seen this with family members, we've seen this with world leaders, and we read about it throughout scripture. Let's look at a few examples.

David was the ninth child born to Jesse of Bethlehem. At a very young age, he was handpicked by the Lord to be the next king of Israel. Yet he was faced with a life-altering decision on the same day he was anointed as the chosen king. God sent Samuel to the house of Jesse to make the selection. Jesse overlooked David and lined up his other sons for Samuel to see. Only when Samuel passed over each of Jesse's sons did Jesse call for David, who was out in the fields tending sheep. In this moment David had a choice to make, and his decision would have either positive or negative consequences. He could have viewed himself as overlooked by his father; the affirmation of a father is so important in a young boy's life. Jesse's actions could have wounded David, causing young David's life to spiral out of control. However, David chose to view himself as handpicked by the Lord. He was the one chosen as the next king of God's people. Instead of allowing that day to lead to a negative consequence, he embraced it and went on to accomplish great things.

Fast-forward several years to when David was king. One day while the army was in battle, David went for a stroll on his rooftop. While enjoying the beautiful day, he happened to notice something even more beautiful. He spotted another man's wife bathing herself across the way. It just so happened David knew the husband and knew he was away in battle. Again, it was decision time for David, with massive consequences waiting on the other side of his decision. This time he failed. David called for Bathsheba to come over, and he had sex with her. To make matters worse, David ended up having her husband killed to cover things up. Bad choices lead to bad consequences. This decision would haunt David for the rest of his life. His son died shortly after being born. He deeply regretted his actions, but it was too late. David had to live with the consequences.

Earlier, in chapter 2, we briefly discussed Joshua and his obedience in taking the city of Jericho. Joshua 6:24 tells us that "they burned the whole city and everything in it, but they put the silver and the gold and the articles of bronze and iron into the treasury of the Lord's house." Then comes the first verse of chapter 7: "But the Israelites acted unfaithfully in regard to the devoted things." Allow me to introduce you to a man named Achan. He was the son of Carmi and was of the tribe of Judah. He was part of the Israelite army. And he decided to take some of the spoils for himself. The Bible tells us that because of Achan's decision, the Lord's anger burned against Israel. The poor decision had been made. Ready for the consequence? The Israelites were preparing to go and take Ai next. Joshua had scoped them out. This would be an easy victory. He only sent a few thousand men because Ai didn't have many men there. Because Achan's decision had caused the Lord to be angry, Israel was thoroughly whipped. They lost thirty-six men and were chased away from the city. Poor decisions are costly. And they affect everyone around us.

Surrendering to WIN

How about Esau from the Old Testament? You may remember him as the boy who sold his birthright for a hearty meal. Esau was an outdoorsman. He was a man's man. One day he came inside starving. All he could think about was filling his belly. I like to eat, so I can relate to the pain he was probably feeling. But giving up his birthright? Bad decision. He traded a long-term blessing for short-term pleasure. He gave up many rights as Isaac's firstborn for a bowl of stew. Sounds crazy, doesn't it? But we do it all the time.

In a vulnerable moment, we too often make poor choices. Choices that affect our health. Choices that affect our families. Choices that affect our well-being. And then we must suffer the consequences. For Esau, the ultimate consequence was huge. Jacob received the birthright. Later, Jacob received his father's blessing. And many years later, the Messiah was born through the lineage of Jacob. Oh, what could have been for Esau! We have no idea what God can do in and through us when we make biblically wise decisions.

It would be unfair to only talk about the negative consequences of bad decisions. Facing a decision that clearly has a wrong path is also an opportunity to do the right thing. And making the right decisions usually leads us to where God wants to take us. As a matter of fact, the very best way to know we are in the center of God's will is to surrender every day and every decision to him. When we are obedient to his word and lay every decision at his feet, he will lead us to the life he has for us. This is a powerful truth. Consider another example from the Old Testament, that of a man named Joseph. Let's begin with the time when he was just a boy. Joseph was the eleventh of twelve sons born to Jacob. Joseph held a special place in the heart of his father, which did not sit well with his brothers. His brothers plotted to kill him but ultimately ended up selling him into slavery in Egypt.

Over a period of several years, Joseph remained faithful to God and continued to make the right decisions. Two instances

CHOICES AND CONSEQUENCES

stand out above the others. Potiphar, one of Pharaoh's officials, purchased Joseph and put him in charge of his entire household. Joseph's complete and total surrender to God's plan for his life was paying off. Genesis 39:2 states, "The Lord was with Joseph, and he prospered." Enter Potiphar's wife. She noticed that Joseph was young, strong, and handsome. She desired to be with him. Imagine young Joseph in this difficult moment of decision. Given that she was the wife of a high-ranking official, she was likely very attractive. He could have very easily given in to his lustful desires and slept with her. But young Joseph was mature beyond his years. And his heart was fully surrendered to God. He resisted her advances, but she lied about what took place. This caused Joseph to end up in prison. But he had made the right decision, and God honored it. Genesis 39:21 tells us, "The Lord was still with him; he showed him kindness and granted him favor in the eyes of the prison warden." And before long he was in charge of the prisoners. God honors decisions that are in line with his will for our lives.

There is also a great stewardship lesson to be learned from young Joseph. When Potiphar brought Joseph in, he noticed the Lord was with him and had given him success in all his endeavors. So Potiphar put Joseph in charge of his entire household and "entrusted to his care everything he owned." Joseph was a faithful steward. He managed the household of Potiphar to the best of his ability. And God blessed his efforts. Genesis 39:5 says, "From the time he put Joseph in charge of his household and of all that he owned, the Lord blessed the household of the Egyptian because of Joseph. The blessing of the Lord was on everything Potiphar had, both in the house and in the field." God not only blessed Joseph, but he also blessed Potiphar and all his affairs as a result of Joseph's faithful stewardship. And when Potiphar's wife made advances on Joseph? It was stewardship that kept Joseph out of trouble. Genesis 39:8–10 says, "But he refused. 'With me in charge,' he told her, 'my master does not concern himself with anything in the house; everything he owns he has entrusted to my care. No one is greater in this house than I am. My master has withheld nothing from me except you, because you are his wife. How then could I do such a wicked thing and sin against God?' And though she spoke to Joseph day after day, he refused to go to bed with her or even be with her." Joseph had been given a great responsibility. He took his management of Potiphar's affairs very seriously, and he made the right decision.

The second time we see Joseph make the right decision and reap positive consequences is when his brothers come to Egypt needing food. Here are a few important background facts. Joseph had worked himself into a position of authority over the entire land of Egypt. God was also working behind the scenes to place Joseph in this prominent position. There were seven years of plenty in the land, which would be followed by seven years of famine. So, food was at a premium. Joseph had access to it. His brothers…not so much. You can see where this is headed. The same brothers who despised him and sold him into slavery come calling in need of food. How easy would it have been for him to exact his revenge at this time? How fitting to starve his brothers and get back at them for what they had done to him? But, again, we see Joseph do the right thing.

Joseph applied the "What would Jesus do?" question thousands of years before its time. He went above and beyond in his service to his brothers, leading to a sweet reunion of the family, including Dad. His brothers were terrified when they found out it was the brother whom they had mistreated who was taking care of them. But Joseph immediately put them at ease and gave God the glory. In Genesis 45:5 he says, "And now do not be distressed and do not be angry with yourselves for selling me here, because it was to save lives that God sent me ahead of you." Isn't that a great attitude? Joseph didn't blame his brothers. He gave God credit for placing him in a position of being able to help. Joseph's life wasn't all about him. He was fully surrendered to God's plan. His heart's desire was to be a faithful steward of all God had entrusted to him. And time and time again, God honored his decisions. Joseph would later tell his brothers that although they had meant what they had done for evil, God had meant it for good. That's the way God works. He works all things together for good. But first, we must be obedient and surrender our decisions to him. He alone is in control.

The last decision I want to discuss was made over two thousand years ago. It was a decision that changed the world. The decision was difficult, painful, and cost a man his life. It was the most selfless act in the history of the world, yet it carried with it the most positive consequence of any decision ever made. Jesus, the Son of God, made a decision to come to earth and die for our sins. As a result of his decision, salvation is available to all who believe. The positive impact of Jesus's sacrifice is still strongly felt today. His decision required him to leave the splendor of heaven and become a helpless baby born in a manger. It meant he would have to suffer and be tortured. It meant he would be made fun of and spit on. It meant he would be mocked and laughed at. It meant he would be stripped naked and humiliated. Yet he made the decision anyway.

We can feel his pain and grief when we hear him say, "My God, My God! Why have you forsaken me?" But a different verse (Luke 22:42) tells the story of his attitude: "not my will but yours (God) be done." Jesus knew what he had to do. Because he loved us so much, he chose to die.

In the final moments before he went to the cross, Jesus faced what would have been the hardest decision in the world for us. He had the power to stop it. He could have called ten thousand angels to help him. He could have struck dead everyone involved in his crucifixion. Jesus had the power to speak himself straight out of the trouble he was in. Yet he made the decision to suffer, bleed, and die for you. And for me. And even for the ones nailing him to the cross. I don't know about you, but I am eternally grateful for the decisions of my Savior. I have hope only because he didn't do what you or I would have done. Jesus surrendered to his assignment. Without this great sacrifice, we would be hopelessly lost. Because of this great sacrifice, we can experience victory.

Hopefully this reminder of the decision Jesus made for us will put our daily decisions in perspective. According to research, we make around thirty-five thousand decisions per day.[1] Some of these are decisions that require little to no thought. Some of these require thought but don't have severe consequences. And then there are the biggies. When we find ourselves at the crossroads of a decision with life-altering consequences, may we be like our Lord and Savior and push forward in the right direction no matter how difficult it may seem. May we be like Joshua who, in his final days, challenged the people of Israel with these words in verse fifteen of chapter twenty-four: "As for me and my household, we will serve the Lord." May we learn from men like David, Achan, and Esau that one bad decision can totally derail God's plan for our life. The surrendered life lays these decisions at the feet of Jesus and prays for guidance. There are other things we can do as well to ensure our decisions line up with God's plan for our lives.

Some decisions have to be made in the spur of the moment. We don't have time to give them a lot of thought and follow a decision-making process. For those decisions, I have a suggestion: make some decisions in advance of the decision. I call these "no matter whats." A few examples of this are: I'm never going to be alone in a closed room with someone of the opposite sex (unless

---

[1] Eva Krockow, "How Many Decisions Do We Make Each Day?" (psychologytoday.com, September 27, 2018).

CHOICES AND CONSEQUENCES

it's my spouse). I'm never going to spend more than $250 without sleeping on it and talking it over with my spouse. I'm not going to set foot in (you name the place) because of the temptation to sin. You get the point. Good decision-making begins well in advance of the actual decision, especially for those "Esau moments" when you do not have time to weigh your options.

For the big decisions in life, here are a few basic steps to take to ensure the right choice is made.

1) **Define and analyze the decision.** What is it you are trying to decide? What are the alternatives? What is the best-case scenario? How about the worst-case scenario? Logically thinking through each point helps you arrive at the best conclusion. Also, make sure to analyze your decision through an eternal lens.
2) **Pray.** The Bible tells us not to worry about anything but to pray about everything. It also says in James 1:5 to ask for wisdom and that God will give it liberally. Going before the Lord with a big decision and surrendering it to him is a critical part of making wise choices.
3) **Apply scripture.** Do one of your options violate scripture? If so, the decision becomes easy. God will not lead you into something in direct conflict with his word. Make sure the path you choose doesn't go against him and his commands. There are also examples in scripture of many decisions we must make in life. Search the Bible and see if someone else has already faced the choice you are facing.
4) **Seek wise counsel.** It is always helpful to talk things out with a trusted friend, counselor, or adviser. Many times we can solve our own dilemmas just by talking through them with someone. But, more importantly,

others can see things we can't see and help us view decisions through a different lens. Proverbs 19:20 tells us to listen to advice and accept instruction and in the end we will be wise. Seeking another opinion before making a big decision shows wisdom and maturity.

5) **Run a "peace test."** This one is simple. Do I have complete peace about it? If the answer is no, then many times it's better to go the other direction. God gives us the Holy Spirit to lead us and to guide us. When that still-small voice is whispering something to us, we are wise to listen and heed the instruction. Pastor Andy Stanley takes this to another level by asking one simple question: "Based on my past experience, current circumstances, and future hopes and dreams, what is the wise thing for me to do?"

One final thing on decision-making. Part of being a mature Christian (and part of our growth process) is being willing to accept the consequences of the decisions we make. Unfortunately, this isn't the norm in our society. We are quick to pass blame and are slow to own up to our poor choices. We find ways to justify any action that doesn't turn out well. And if we can find someone else to pin the blame on, then so be it. As followers of Jesus, we should prayerfully consider each choice that is set before us. But when a wrong decision is made, let's do all we can to own it, make it right, learn from it, and move on. Surrendering is a choice. Being a good steward is a choice. In this next chapter, we will look at how we can surrender our time to him, make every decision count, and win the time-management battle.

CHOICES AND CONSEQUENCES

Simple Summary

1) All choices (both good and bad) have consequences (either positive or negative).

2) The choices you make determine the direction of your life.

3) The Bible gives us many examples of both good and bad decisions.

4) You can do a few practical things to help you make wise decisions.

5) Part of being a mature Christian is being willing to accept the consequences of the choices we make.

Chapter 5

STEWARDING TIME WISELY

*Teach us to number our days
that we may gain a heart of wisdom.*
—Psalm 90:12

We live in a very distracted world. It seems that every minute of every day brings a new demand for our time, energy, and attention. One of the biggest reasons we make poor choices is because we are constantly bombarded with messages from the world around us. If we are going to win the time-management battle and surrender our time to the Lord, we must be very intentional. We need to have a plan and, more importantly, the discipline to carry it out.

Again, hear the words of Scott Rodin:

> Today we are in an era when we are in bondage to time. Our entire lives are controlled by the clock and we just do not have the freedom to do the things we know to be right because of the watch on our hands. The Kenyans have the following saying to express this western culture, "Westerners are people with gods on their wrists."
>
> We need to be delivered from this bondage if we are to be good stewards for God's kingdom. If we have to apply

the parable of the Good Samaritan in our lives today, we cannot be Good Samaritans because we have gods sitting on our wrists. For the Good Samaritan to do what he did, he needed to forget his appointments and recognize the opportunity that God had brought before him to serve the wounded man.[1]

Here is the reality: we all have twenty-four hours each day to do what needs to be done. "I don't have time for (fill in the blank)" is just an excuse we use when something isn't really a priority. We make time for the things in life we care about. We are all filling our schedules with something. What is that something for you?

Deep down in the heart of every person lies a desire for their life to count for something. To achieve maximum kingdom impact with our lives, we must win some daily battles. I am going to begin with a few of the biggest hurdles we face in our struggle to make our time count.

Smartphones

Never before has so much information been available to us at just the click of a button. We can check the weather, our email, or what our neighbor had for breakfast from a handheld device we call a smartphone. These gadgets have all but taken over the technological world. And it's scary how close we are to removing the word technological from that last sentence! Everywhere you go, faces are buried in the screen of a phone, and its owner is completely oblivious to the world around him. Before I express my concern about our addiction to our cell phones, I will say that there are a lot of advantages this type of technology brings us. It's not all bad. Advances in technology have improved our lives in many ways. It's obvious we believe that; just look at the multibillion-dollar industry created from this revolution. Apple iPhones alone

---

[1] Scott Rodin, *The Steward's Journey*, Stewardship of Our Time. https://thestewardsjourney.com/stewardship-of-our-time/

STEWARDING TIME WISELY

in 2017 moved off the shelves to the tune of $1.5 billion worth of product. So that you will know where I am coming from, let me give you a little background as to how my viewpoint was shaped.

I grew up in a small town in rural Mississippi at a time when Steve Jobs and Bill Gates were just getting started. Our first computer was a Tandy 1000 that moved at the speed of a turtle with a broken leg. We didn't surf the internet with it. Instead we played games like three-dimensional tic-tac-toe and *Earl Weaver Baseball* (bet you baseball fans haven't heard that name in a long time!). Our home phone was a landline that was shared by three other families on our street. How do you think that would work today? Imagine picking up your cell phone but having to immediately hang up because someone else was already using it!

Social media didn't exist. The media that kept us "socially informed" came to us every day around 3:00 p.m. in the form of the *Hattiesburg American* newspaper. Our family would sit around the living room and pass the paper around one section at a time. Sounds almost silly, but life was so simple then. If the phone rang, it never crossed my mind that it might be for me. I never thought about our phone. To "check the phone" two-thousand-plus times a day would have been absurd. To put it in my pocket and carry it around with me all day would have probably resulted in someone scheduling an appointment for me with my Uncle Larry, who was a psychiatrist. Things were just different then. I might even argue that things were better.

Fast-forward to today. Studies show that the average smartphone owner checks their phone every twelve minutes. That translates to eighty times per day.[2] We touch, swipe, or click our screens 2,617 times every single day.[3] Are you kidding me? We

---

2 SWNS, "Americans Check Their Phones 80 Times per Day," (nypost.com, November 8, 2017).
3 Julia Naftulan, "Here's How Many Times We Touch Our Phone Every Day," (Businessinsider.com, July 13, 2016).

spend over two and a half hours on social media each day.[4] For most people, their phone is the last thing they see at night and the first thing they check when they wake up. We have created an unhealthy habit of depending on our smartphones for everything. They tell us about the weather, who won the game last night, how to get where we are going, and what the stock market did that day. We depend on them so much that laws have now been passed to require us to at least put them down while we are driving. If you look around you, you will see these laws are being violated by a large number of drivers. Families no longer talk and interact at the dinner table or in restaurants. Instead, everyone is playing with their phones.

We are now on call for every contact in our phones 24-7. This includes phone calls, text messages, Facebook messages, emails—the list goes on and on. No wonder we don't have time for Bible study! No wonder we don't have time to be productive at work! No wonder families are being torn apart! We have traded deep, meaningful relationships for Facebook friends! Ok, I'm sorry. I got a little carried away, but you can see I am passionate about this. If we are going to manage our time wisely and have our lives count for something, we must find ways to disconnect and take back control of our lives. Otherwise, there will always be something or someone filling our hours for us.

Television

About ten years ago, I became really convicted that I was watching too much football. Aubrey and I didn't have kids at the time, so my football weekends started on Thursday night at six-thirty and didn't end until Monday night at eleven. On Saturdays I would literally watch football from 11:00 a.m. to 11:00 p.m. And poor Aubrey was such a trooper. She knew how much I loved it, so she

---

4 Saima Salim, "How Much Time Do You Spend on Social Media?" (Digital Information World, January 4, 2019).

never complained and even joined me in watching a game or two. Somewhere around that same time, a friend of mine introduced me to a man who would change my life. Ok, that might be a slight exaggeration. His name was Jack Bauer. If you know who he is, you probably just shouted "Amen!" For the rest of you, Jack Bauer was a man who protected our country from terrorists and kept multiple presidents from being assassinated. He was the star of the TV show *24*. And he was one bad dude. Along with football and *24*, we also had a few other things we watched. So, yes, we spent a lot of time staring at our television screen.

God really began to convict me about this, so I set out to change. I wish I could tell you I immediately began substituting God-honoring activities for my TV-watching time, but that wasn't the case. Nothing really changed until January 10, 2012. That's the day our twin boys, Max and Miles, arrived, turning Daddy and Mommy's world upside down. I wanted desperately to be a good father, so I made a decision when the boys were born: instead of watching meaningless, mind-numbing TV, I would begin reading books that helped me become a better version of myself. When I had free time (which wasn't often for the first year of their lives), I would resist the urge to turn on the television and instead pick up a book. I read books on parenting and marriage. I read books on being a better man and a better Christian. I read books on leadership and church growth. I read business books and books on how to build better relationships. And what I found out during this time was I loved reading!

Slowly, over time, I found myself looking forward to reading (a good use of my time) more than watching television (mostly a waste of my time). I can truly say that intentional time-management decision changed my life. The information going into my mind from a great Christian book is far superior to the messages being sent to me by a TV show or even a football game (have you watched the commercials lately?). I learned to be intentional about investing my time wisely.

I share my story with you because I don't believe I'm the only one who has struggled with wasting time in front of the television screen. Don't get me wrong here. I'm not saying family movie night or enjoying a good show with your spouse is a bad thing. I'm talking about losing yourself for countless hours in a semi-comatose state while being entertained the world's way. I think in today's terminology it's called a "Netflix binge." The average American spends nearly six hours each day watching television. How are we even productive as a country? If you want to make your time on this earth count for something and be a kingdom player that God can count on, you must be way below that average.

Video Games

Along the same lines as watching too much television is the new addiction we seem to have to playing video games. Recently I walked into a local electronics store with my two little boys. They had received a gift certificate for their birthday and wanted to see what was available. As I was walking down the aisle, I ran into a guy I knew but hadn't seen in a while. When I asked him how he and his family were doing, he immediately launched into a passionate explanation of each video game he was playing and which ones he had mastered.

I was caught off guard, to say the least. This gentleman was in his thirties and had two children! He told me about his impressive collection of every gaming unit and popular games dating back to the 1980s. He asked me several questions that I had absolutely no answer for. I haven't played video games regularly since college! While these games can be fun, they are a giant time waster. Be careful to not get sucked into this trap. And if you have children, guardrails need to be placed around them as well.

Social Media

Since we've already covered smartphones, we will not spend a lot of time here. Social media has become the number one use of the cell phone. That's right. We are no longer using our phones for calling. We use them to see what the rest of the world is up to. Whether it's Twitter, Facebook, Instagram, Snapchat, or some other form of social media, our culture has become obsessed with it. I mentioned earlier that the average person spends two and a half hours per day on social media. Considering that a day has only sixteen waking hours, that number is hard to imagine. Again, I'm not saying social media is evil. I'm simply warning you that it can be a giant time waster. Here are a few warning signs that you might be overusing social media:

1) If you find yourself scrolling through social media at red lights, the dinner table, or anytime you have forty-five seconds of down time, it might be a problem.
2) If your mood is determined by the things you see or read on social media, you probably need to distance yourself from it.
3) If your primary form of communication with the world around you (including friends and family) is through social media, it might be time to reevaluate your use of it.

As in anything else, moderation is the key. Social media can be fun, entertaining, and in some cases very useful. Just don't abuse it. God doesn't care how many Facebook friends or Twitter followers you have. He cares that you are being a good steward of the time he gives you every single day. So what does that look like? I'm glad you asked.

"The greatest use of this life is to spend it on something that will outlast it." I love that quote from William James! Here is the reality of time management: our lives and our time will be invested in *something*. There is no way to escape this basic truth. I learned a long time ago in Economics 101 the definition of opportunity cost—a decision to do one thing is a decision not to do something else. So what are the things we can invest our time in today that will outlast our lives on this earth? What are the things that really and truly matter? Allow me to summarize the best options.

1) **Time with God.** This is a must! Whether you call it quiet time, prayer time, or a time of meditation, it is extremely important to spend time alone in prayer and Bible study each day.
2) **Time with others.** In this busy world where we have limited time and unlimited demands, making time for those we love is so important. We must be intentional about giving our family, spouses, and children something other than our leftovers.
3) **Time with self.** Yes, spending time working on you is important. Maybe this is reading. Maybe it is exercise. Maybe it's another hobby that recharges your batteries. Whatever that looks like for you, it is vital to have this time each day. I call it sharpening the saw. You can't help someone else cut down their tree if your saw is dull. Spend time working on you. Let's break it down even further. Below are two primary focuses that will allow you to spend your life on something that will outlast it.

Relationships

At the end of everyone's life, there are only two things that matter: "What did I do *with* Jesus?" and "What did I do *for* Jesus?" The first question speaks to your salvation (see chapter 3). The next question for the most part deals with the second greatest commandment: love your neighbor as yourself. We all love ourselves. But we were created for relationships with others. At the risk of sounding a bit morbid, I have a question for you: What will people say about you at your funeral? Were you kind and loving to those who knew you best? Will you leave behind a number of deep, meaningful relationships? When we are on our death beds, we will not ask for our riches or possessions to be brought into the room. We will not ask the doctor if we can make one more trip to the office. No, we will want those we love around us until the very end.

My father worked for a ruthless businessman for thirty-five years. He always put the bottom line ahead of the person helping him drive it. One day he called my dad into his office and told him that he would have to pay folks to come to his funeral and carry his casket because he had driven away all his friends. How sad. You can avoid being like this gentleman by simply investing in your precious relationships while you still have time.

If you are married, love and serve your spouse faithfully "until death do ye part." If you have children, don't neglect them. Spend as much time with them as possible and create as many memories with them as you can. Get to know people around you and make as many friends as you can. Treat everyone you meet with kindness and respect. Pour out love every day to everyone you meet. And if you have questions about what it looks like to invest in relationships, go study the life and ministry of Jesus.

Kingdom Activities

C. T. Studd was quoted as saying, "Only one life, twill soon be past, only what is done for Christ will last." This is so true. Every thought, word, and deed here on this earth is being recorded. One day we will meet the King of Kings and give an account of what we did with our lives. So if you want to invest your time into something that will outlast you, consider Christ centered-activities that have a kingdom impact. Entire books have been written on this subject, so I won't go into great detail. Just know this. The Bible is very clear that we have the ability to "store up treasures in Heaven." It is also very clear on the fact that we are called to share the Gospel and make disciples. When we surrender our lives to God and join in where he is at work, our lives take on new meaning. Whether it is serving in the local church, going on a mission trip, or simply baking bread for a widow, God notices when we are obedient. Time spent in prayer or Bible study strengthens our relationship with God. We can't meet every need nor say yes to everything, but God can and will use you if you just make yourself available.

Our time on earth is very limited. If we are going to accomplish all God has for us, we must immediately begin cutting out "time wasters" and adding "kingdom builders" to our schedule. I can't tell you exactly what this looks like for you. Maybe it is trading NFL football on a Sunday afternoon for a service opportunity with your church. Maybe it is putting down your cell phone and spending more time with your children. Or maybe it is using your vacation days to go on an international mission trip. Let me encourage you to surrender your time to the Lord and invest it in things he wants you to do.

I also want to mention another excellent use of time. I am probably preaching to the choir here since you have purchased a copy of this book. But I am referring to *reading*. Picking up a good book and using it for knowledge, encouragement, or motivation is definitely time well spent. Our minds are like computers. Garbage in, garbage out. The input into our brains program how we think and behave. This makes reading God's word and good Christian writings so important. If you begin investing your time reading the Bible and other Christian books, your heart will slowly be transformed. I'm not talking about romance novels or James Patterson murder mysteries. I'm talking about the writings of some of the great modern-day Christian leaders like David Platt, Francis Chan, Max Lucado, Rick Warren, and John Piper. You get the idea here.

In closing, there is a powerful story told of the final days of Alexander the Great. As a reminder of who he was, Alexander was king of the ancient Greek kingdom of Macedon from 336–323 BC. He succeeded his father, Philip, taking over the throne

STEWARDING TIME WISELY

at the age of twenty. Alexander was a great military leader and is widely considered one of the most influential people in history. In his last days, as he lay helpless in his bed waiting to breathe his last breath, he called in his generals. His request was simple and consisted of three parts. They were as follows:

1) "My first desire," said Alexander, "is that my physicians alone must carry my coffin."
2) After a pause he continued, "Secondly, I desire that when my coffin is being carried to the grave, the path leading to the graveyard be strewn with gold, silver, and precious stones that I have collected in my treasury."
3) The king felt exhausted after saying this. He took a minute's rest and continued, "My third and last wish is that both my hands be kept dangling out of my coffin."

The people who had gathered there wondered at the king's strange wishes. But no one dared bring the question to their lips. Alexander's favorite general kissed his hands and pressed them to his heart. "O king, we assure you that all your wishes will be fulfilled. But tell us, why do you make such strange wishes?"

At this, Alexander took a deep breath and said,

> I would like the world to know of the three lessons I have just learned. I want my physicians to carry my coffin because people should realize that no doctor on this earth can really cure anybody. They are powerless and cannot save a person from the clutches of death. So, let not people take life for granted.
>
> The second wish of strewing gold, silver, and other riches on the path to the graveyard is meant to tell people that not even a fraction of gold will come with me. I spent all my life being greedy and earning riches but cannot take anything with me. Let people realize that it is a sheer waste of time to chase wealth.

About my third wish of having my hands dangling out of the coffin, I wish people to know that I came empty handed into this world and empty handed I go out of this world.[5]

Friends, each moment of time on this earth is precious. We can live for ourselves or we can live for a cause that is greater than us. Job said it best when he proclaimed that he arrived on this planet naked and naked will he return. But we have a golden opportunity while we are here to make a difference with the time we are given. Being a good steward of our time means focusing on the things that matter.

Simple Summary

1) We must be very intentional if we want to use our time wisely.

2) Cell phones, televisions, and other forms of technology can be massive time wasters.

3) The greatest use of our time is to spend it on things that will outlast us.

4) Relationships and kingdom activities are two great investments of time.

5) Our time on earth is limited and precious. We must make each day count.

---

5 Alexander the Great, *The Last 3 Wishes of Alexander the Great* (positive thinking.in).

Section 2:
Our Talents

Chapter 6

WHO AM I?

*For we are God's handiwork,
created in Christ Jesus to do good works
which God prepared in advance for us to do.*
—Ephesians 2:10

What started out as a typical day for Moses tending sheep for his father-in-law ended up being the day that would forever change his life. As he watched a flaming bush not burn to the ground, he had to go over and see what was going on. It was there that God issued a direct command for Moses to go to Pharaoh and bring his people out of Egypt. As would have been the case for many of us, Moses's first response to this assignment was not one to be proud of. His initial response can be found in Exodus 3:11: "*Who am I* that I should go to Pharaoh and bring the Israelites out of Egypt?"

Who am I? That is a question we all ask ourselves at some point in our lives. We could, like Moses, be asking because of doubt, which is a common emotion when faced with a daunting task. But a healthier reason to ask this question is to gain a better understanding of how God made us. Our Lord wants us to know who we are in him.

It is much easier to spend time wisely when you know who you are. Knowing your strengths allows you to know what to say

Surrendering to WIN

yes to. If you know the areas in which you are weak or not gifted, saying no becomes much easier. Also, knowing who you are in Christ gives your life hope, purpose, and meaning. Let's start with the basics. If you are a follower of Jesus, you can answer the "Who am I?" question with the following answer: I am created in the image of almighty God. I am the crown of his creation. I am fearfully and wonderfully made. I was knit perfectly together in my mother's womb before I was born. I am his masterpiece! I am a child of the one true King, and I am heir to the throne that will reign eternally. That's who I am!

Wow! When you think about that response, it should put a little extra pep in your steps. We are each unique creations placed on this earth to fulfill a special assignment. No one else can fill the role of me or you. Dr. Seuss said it best when he stated, "Today you are you. That is truer than true. There is no one alive more you-er than you!" That's exciting! Whether we feel special or not, when we wake up every day, we have a unique assignment. We have a race to run that is set before us one day at a time. A God-ordained assignment is given to us based on our strengths, personalities, and unique influences. What an awesome thought! All that is required of us is the desire to understand who we are and the perseverance to keep taking the next step in our race. Let's take a minute to unpack the previous "who I am" statement.

I am created in the image of almighty God. In the first few chapters of the book of Genesis, God creates the heavens and the earth. He creates the birds of the air and the beasts of the field. He creates the sun and moon and the land and sea. Then something special happens. God creates man. The Bible tells us in Genesis 1:27, "God created mankind in His own image, in the image of God He created them, male and female He created them." God made man and gave him power over the earth. We were different than the animals. We were to rule over them. We were set on the earth to "subdue it," which means it became our dominion to

WHO AM I?

oversee. We were special from the beginning based on the position God had put us in.

But if that is not enough, look again at the words of Genesis 1:27: *"in His own image He created them."* I'm sorry to continue using the same word over and over, but *wow*! That's the only word that can adequately describe what we are reading. The Creator of all things decided we were so special we should look like him. He entrusted his image and likeness to mankind and set us on earth to make a God-inspired difference. We were created on purpose for a purpose. That's pretty cool. This makes us the crown of his creation. Nothing else that was created in those six days resembled God. Everything created reflected his glory, but nothing else bore his image. It is evident from these early chapters of the Bible that man was God's most important creation. This means our lives have meaning and purpose from the day we are born until the day he takes us home. We were created to be winners. We are image-bearers of almighty God. That's who we are. Wow!

Psalm 139:13–14 says, "For you created my inmost being; you knit me together in my mother's womb. I praise you because I am fearfully and wonderfully made." God knew about me before I even entered this world. He had a plan for my life when I was just a gleam in my daddy's eye. I love this picture of being "knit together" before I was born. My great-grandmother loved to sew. She would spend countless hours sitting in her recliner carefully constructing the design of a quilt or dress or other garment. Every pull of the thread through a loop or movement of the needle had meaning. The masterpiece she was creating required careful planning and patient execution of her sewing skills. The end result would be a one-of-a-kind product with a specific purpose. That's us! God handcrafted our unique design. Here are a few interesting facts about the handiwork that is you:

1) Our body is made up of atoms, which are the building blocks for cells.

2) An adult body is made up of seven octillion atoms. That's seven with twenty-seven zeros!
3) Cells are the smallest unit of life in the human body. It is estimated that your body has over one hundred trillion cells!
4) Found inside the cell is DNA. What is DNA? The biological instructions that make you who you are. The blueprint of life and your unique characteristics.
5) If you put all the DNA molecules in your body end to end, the DNA would reach from the earth to the sun and back over six hundred times.
6) Segments of DNA are called genes. Genes are unique traits that are inherited from parents. Humans have approximately thirty thousand genes in their body.
7) A genome is all the DNA in a cell, including the genes.
8) It would take fifty years to type the entire human genome if someone typed at a speed of sixty words per minute and worked eight hours a day![1]

Isn't that cool? Don't ever think for one second that you are not important. Ephesians 2:10 tells us that we are God's workmanship (handiwork, masterpiece), created for good works that he prepared *in advance* for us to do. God has a plan for you and for me. That is why he breathed life into us. Embrace this great truth.

When I was a little boy, one of my permanent teeth never came in. My orthodontist put braces on my teeth to pull them together and cover the gap from the missing tooth. He then filed a tooth down to make it look like the missing tooth. Perfect! My mouth now looked normal. Fast-forward almost twenty years to the night I met my wife. She was supposed to be introduced to

---

[1] Public Broadcasting Station, "Cracking the Code of Life: Genome Facts" (pbs.org, 2001).

my brother that night. God had other plans. Aubrey walks up to our group, looks at me, and blurts out, "You are missing a lateral."

"Excuse me?" was my response.

"Your teeth—it looks like you have one that isn't there."

"How did you know that?" I asked.

"Because I am a dental hygienist," she replied.

"I'm Neal; very nice to meet you, Ms. Dental Hygienist!"

What I had viewed as a physical flaw for twenty years was the one thing that caught the attention of the lady I've now been married to for fifteen years. Isn't God good? We are his masterpiece. He created us just the way he wanted us. There are no mistakes in God's design. He has a plan, and every detail matters in his kingdom.

Lastly, you are a child of the one true King, which means you are an heir to the throne above all thrones. This one is so powerful and so awesome our tiny brains cannot comprehend all that is being said here. We've already established the fact that God owns it all. If he owns it all and I am his heir, then I stand to benefit from the inheritance of my father. What is his will one day be mine! I belong to the kingdom that wins in the end. That's pretty cool.

In my current occupation, I spend a good bit of time helping people with what I call "legacy planning." As they get older, my clients start thinking more about death and the type of legacy they will leave for their children and grandchildren. Naming beneficiaries of investment accounts and other assets is a big part of this type of planning. When a son or daughter is listed as the beneficiary of the account, that money is passed directly to them when Dad or Mom passes away. Pretty basic stuff, right? What I am about to share next is anything but basic. When we who are followers of Jesus pass away, we will step into an inheritance unlike anything we could ever imagine. Heaven awaits those of us who profess Jesus as Lord. The best way I could tell you about heaven is to share the following story.

Surrendering to WIN

A rich man was determined to take all his wealth with him when he passed away. So he liquidated all his assets, bought blocks of gold, and bagged them all up to hang onto until death. When he died, he was met at heaven's gates by Saint Peter. "I will have to check that bag out before I let you in," said Saint Peter. After looking at the contents of the bag, Saint Peter asked the man with a confused face, "Why in the world are you trying to sneak asphalt into heaven?"

The streets in heaven will be paved with pure gold. The sights, smells, and sounds are beyond what "any eye has seen or ear has heard." The mansions being prepared for us will blow us away. When Jesus says, "I am going to prepare a place for you," there is no telling what he has in mind. We have so much to look forward to on the other side. As children of the King of Kings, our inheritance is waiting on us. We will enjoy it forever and ever. When life starts beating you down, remind yourself of this great truth: My Heavenly Father is the Great I Am. My identity is found in him and him alone. This world cannot and will not convince me otherwise.

Switching gears for just a few minutes, there are two other unique traits that God has given you: your personality type and your spiritual gifts. Let's start with personality type.

Over the years I have really enjoyed studying and learning about how differently people are "wired." I think everyone would agree that our personalities are similar to those of some people we know and totally different from those of others. Recently the enneagram test has become a favorite for understanding one's natural bend. It is a personality test made popular by a gentleman named Oscar Ichazo in the 1960s. Although some argue its origin dates back to much earlier than that, Ichazo taught it in schools and helped it gain popularity. The test focuses on nine personality types and assigns a number to each. It is a fun, easy way to help you better understand yourself and why you think and act

WHO AM I?

the way you do. For more information on this, read the book *The Road Back to You* by Ian Morgan Cron and Suzanne Stabile.

I'm not going to spend a lot of time on this topic here, but I will share my favorite version of personality tests that categorize people. It is called the people puzzle. It was developed by Dr. Tony Alessandra and is quite simple to understand.

There are four basic personality types:

Thinker: analytical, likes details, enjoys data, systematic, likes time for themselves, works slowly, careful planner, likes organization and structure, problem solver

Director: firm, goal oriented, likes to be productive, competitive, bottom line–focused, more guarded, impatient, makes things happen, usually more direct, achiever

Relator: caring, warm, open in relationships, compassionate, loving, supportive and reliable, more emotional, good listener, dislikes conflict

Socializer: very open, fun, dreamer, spontaneous, lives for the moment, creative, enjoys people, works well with others, excitable, persuasive[2]

Which one are you? Knowing your personality can help you better understand how God created you and what he is calling you to do (and not to do). It can also be very helpful in choosing a career and learning how to interact with others. No one personality type is any better than another. Learn who you are, and then embrace the personality type that God gave you.

Let's go back to Moses in the Book of Exodus. In chapter 18 this fearless leader of the Israelites receives a visit from his father-in-law, Jethro. After exchanging pleasantries with Jethro,

---

[2] Tony Alessandra, "People Puzzle" (alessandra.com).

Moses must get back down to business. In verse 13 he takes his seat and begins serving as the judge for the people. It doesn't take Jethro long to intervene. He says in verse 14, " 'What is this you are doing for the people? Why do you alone sit as judge while all these people stand around you from morning until evening?' " Jethro continues in verses 17 and 18: " 'What you are doing is not good! You and these people will only wear yourselves out. The work is too heavy for you. You cannot handle it alone.' "

Jethro called Moses out. He knew Moses well; Moses was a leader. He wasn't a judge. He needed to delegate and not try to do it all himself (sounds like a problem we all struggle with!). Jethro helped him with this. Verse 24 tells us "Moses listened to his father-in-law and did everything he said." No doubt Moses's life thus got much easier. When he embraced his unique design and started operating from his strengths, he and his people thrived. Such is the case with us. We can get bogged down and frustrated when we spend too much time doing things we aren't wired to do. But there is nothing better than spending time in our sweet spot.

The second unique trait we receive from God is our spiritual gifts. If you have never taken a spiritual gifts survey, I encourage you to do so. Several different versions can be found online. The basis for these questionnaires is found in 1 Corinthians 12.

> Now about the gifts of the Spirit, brothers and sisters, I do not want you to be uninformed. You know that when you were pagans, somehow or other you were influenced and led astray to mute idols. Therefore I want you to know that no one who is speaking by the Spirit of God says, "Jesus be cursed," and no one can say, "Jesus is Lord," except by the Holy Spirit.
>
> There are different kinds of gifts, but the same Spirit distributes them. There are different kinds of service, but the same Lord. There are different kinds of working, but in all of them and in everyone it is the same God at work.

WHO AM I?

Now to each one the manifestation of the Spirit is given for the common good. To one there is given through the Spirit a message of wisdom, to another a message of knowledge by means of the same Spirit, to another faith by the same Spirit, to another gifts of healing by that one Spirit, to another miraculous powers, to another prophecy, to another distinguishing between spirits, to another speaking in different kinds of tongues, and to still another the interpretation of tongues. All these are the work of one and the same Spirit, and he distributes them to each one, just as he determines.

Just as a body, though one, has many parts, but all its many parts form one body, so it is with Christ. For we were all baptized by one Spirit so as to form one body—whether Jews or Gentiles, slave or free—and we were all given the one Spirit to drink.

Even so the body is not made up of one part but of many. Now if the foot should say, "Because I am not a hand, I do not belong to the body," it would not for that reason stop being part of the body. And if the ear should say, "Because I am not an eye, I do not belong to the body," it would not for that reason stop being part of the body. If the whole body were an eye, where would the sense of hearing be? If the whole body were an ear, where would the sense of smell be? But in fact God has placed the parts in the body, every one of them, just as he wanted them to be. If they were all one part, where would the body be? As it is, there are many parts, but one body.

The eye cannot say to the hand, "I don't need you!" And the head cannot say to the feet, "I don't need you!" On the contrary, those parts of the body that seem to be weaker are indispensable, and the parts that we think are less honorable we treat with special honor. And the parts that are unpresentable are treated with special modesty, while our presentable parts need no special treatment. But God has put the body together, giving greater honor to the parts that lacked it, so that there should be no division in the body, but that its parts should have equal concern for each other. If one part suffers, every part suffers with it; if one part is honored, every part rejoices with it.

Now you are the body of Christ, and each one of you is a part of it. And God has placed in the church first of all apostles, second prophets, third teachers, then miracles, then gifts of healing, of helping, of guidance, and of different kinds of tongues. Are all apostles? Are all prophets? Are all teachers? Do all work miracles? Do all have gifts of healing? Do all speak in tongues? Do all interpret? Now eagerly desire the greater gifts.

Paul is encouraging each person to use their giftedness to build up the church—the body of Christ. He uses the physical body as an example. When we accept Christ as our Lord and Savior, his spirit comes to live inside of us. The Holy Spirit leads us and guides us along life's journey. The spirit gives us certain gifts or talents to be used to make a kingdom impact. There are others listed in Romans 12:6–8. As you can see, the list is long. Some argue that we are supposed to do all the things listed in 1 Corinthians 12 and Romans 12. This is not a book about spiritual gifts, so I'm not going to address either side of that argument. The bottom line is this: through God's Spirit, he empowers us to play an important role in his kingdom work. While all the gifts listed are good, no one would argue against the fact that you are better at some than others. Which ones come easily to you? Which ones energize you? Which ones have other people affirmed for you? It's important to have a better understanding of how you are gifted and how these gifts can be used for God's glory.

WHO AM I?

So what does this have to do with surrender and stewardship? God gave you your strengths. God gave you your talents. God made you a unique creation and has a unique contribution for you to make here on earth. When you know who you are in Christ and you know exactly how he designed you, it is easy to find his will for your life. But you must surrender. You must lay your gifts and talents at his feet and ask him how to proceed.

Let me give you a personal example. Early in my working career, I recognized that God had given me the gift of communication and connecting with people. *Great*, I thought. *These skills translated perfectly into a sales career where I can make a lot of money!* God then used a Lee Corso line on me: "Not so fast, my friend!" It took me a while to surrender to him, but now I know he also gave me this gift to be used for ministry and pointing people back to him. Make sense?

I mentioned David a few chapters back. David had a strong understanding of his self-worth and who he was even at a young age. When his own father did not consider him for the future king anointing, David wasn't fazed. What could have easily derailed his entire career actually served to strengthen his confidence in how God had created him. Later, when he stepped up to face Goliath, he knew his strengths and what it would take to win the battle. David wasn't a mighty warrior who needed heavy armor for the fight. He was a young shepherd boy who was extremely accurate with a slingshot.

So what are the key takeaways for us:

- We must figure out how we were perfectly (and uniquely) knit together.
- We must surrender that design to him and let him use us to make an eternal difference in the lives of others.
- We must trust God and find our identity in him and him alone.

Surrendering to WIN

For many of us, the playing field for utilizing our giftedness is the place we work. In the next chapter, we will examine how that might look.

Simple Summary

1) Knowing our strengths, weaknesses, and unique wiring makes us more effective in how we impact God's kingdom in a positive way.

2) We are all created in the image of almighty God.

3) We each have different personality types and different spiritual gifts.

4) God has a unique role for each of us that only we can fill.

5) We must surrender our design to the One who created us.

Chapter 7

WINNING AT WORK

Whatever you do, work at it with all your heart as working for the Lord and not for men.
—Colossians 3:23

Work. That word makes some people sick at their stomachs. It makes others smile and gives them energy. Why the difference? Most people have "surrendered" to their work instead of "surrendering" their work. Work has beaten them down and forced them into submission. I am convinced there is a better way. Here are three bottom line facts to consider:

1) Assuming a forty-hour work week, fifty weeks each year, and a forty-year working career, you will spend eighty thousand hours at work.
2) You spend way too much time working to dread it every day and not enjoy it.
3) You also spend way too much of your time at work not to use it as a ministry (more on this later).

Studies show that, unfortunately, most people do not enjoy what they do for a living. In fact, a 2013 Gallop poll stated the number was around 70 percent.[1] And "not enjoy" was not the term used.

---

1 Beth Stebner, "Workplace Morale Heads Down: 70% of Americans Negative about Their Jobs, Gallup Study Shows" (*New York Daily News*, June 24, 2013).

Surrendering to WIN

The word was "hate." According to the *New York Times*, deaths from heart attacks follow a pattern during the week. The lowest risk is on the weekend and the highest risk is on Monday mornings.[2] Work-related stress is a leading contributor to these heart attacks. For several years, suicides rates have been the highest on Sunday nights and Monday mornings due to pressure and stress from job responsibilities. This information leaves me scratching my head. Why would someone stay in a job they hate and risk a heart attack or be driven to contemplate suicide? There are so many different answers to this question, but I will offer my thoughts.

- Most people are afraid of change. Once they are comfortable with the daily requirements and the people around them, change scares them to death.
- Most workers like the security of their job and the steady paycheck it offers. If you've been in a job awhile and have little risk of losing that position, leaving becomes more difficult.
- People believe their degree needs to align with their occupational field. I see this one all the time. If you studied law in school, you are supposed to work forty years as a lawyer, right? Not necessarily. I have a friend who received his doctorate in pharmacy and realized he hated being a pharmacist. After ten years in retail pharmacy, he changed careers.
- A lot of people stay in a job they do not like because of the expectations of others. We do not want to let Dad, Mom, or our spouse down, so we continue working in a job we do not enjoy.
- This last one is the one I see the most—financial obligations. We will discuss this more in chapter 8, but

---

2 Anahad O'Connor, "The Claim: Heart Attacks Are More Common on Mondays" (*New York Times*, March 14, 2006).

here is what I mean: if you have raised your standard of living up to your income level and have no financial margin, you may be forced to continue in a job or career you do not like. Sometimes changing career paths requires a temporary decrease in income. This isn't possible if you are living paycheck to paycheck.

So what is the answer? How can we truly win in the workplace? Surrender. Bringing your work life under the lordship of Creator God is one of the most rewarding things you will ever do. Surrendering this area of your life to him will cause you to ask questions like: Am I doing what God has called me to do? Am I fully utilizing my God-given talents every day? Am I energized and fulfilled in my work or just going through the motions? It will cause you to pray daily prayers like, "God, I want more than anything to be in the center of your will for my life. Please show me what that looks like." Asking these questions and praying these prayers will very likely lead you to rethink your current career path. It could require a giant leap of faith. It certainly did for me. Allow me to share my story with you.

In 2002, I accepted a position as a pharmaceutical sales rep with Eli Lilly and Company. It was a great job, especially for someone straight out of college with no real work experience. Not only did I not have work experience, but I also did not even own a suit! For the interview day, I borrowed my dad's suit and tie, pulled a belt really tight to keep my pants from falling down, and walked into the building like I belonged. God was gracious enough to allow me to get the job. After a couple of years on the job, I began to wonder if this was really what God was calling me to do in the long term. My boredom each day was increasing, and my sense of fulfillment was decreasing. I wanted to make a real difference in people's lives but standing in a medicine closet waiting to get fifteen seconds of a physician's time just wasn't cutting it.

Surrendering to WIN

Thankfully, I had done pretty well and was being noticed by those above me on the corporate ladder. A promotion into something more meaningful was a possibility. In 2007, I received the final stamp of approval to be promoted into a new role on the management career path. The company flew me to their home office in Indianapolis, where I job-shadowed in several different departments. Everyone was excited about me leaving the field and becoming a home office associate. Everyone, that is, except for me! Something just didn't seem right. In my heart of hearts, I felt my time in corporate America was coming to an end. But what would I do? My current compensation package was now six figures, and I had no experience in any other field. At least that's what I thought. God had been preparing me for something that should have been crystal clear to me. I just had not been paying attention because I had been too busy trying to make money and climb the corporate ladder.

When I received my first paycheck in 2002, the reality of now being in the real world smacked me in the face. I was now making my own money and paying my own bills. What do I do? What does this look like? Am I ready for this? Since I was making decent money and had no debt, I embarked on a mission to educate myself. I read personal finance books, attended educational seminars, and picked the brain of anyone in my circle who had achieved success. Before long I had found I really enjoyed the information and even enjoyed sharing it with others. Several friends and coworkers came to me for advice, and I found great satisfaction in helping them.

So, in 2007, when I was at the crossroads of a job promotion or a job change, this is what I did. I prayed. And prayed. And prayed some more. Was God calling me to help people win with money? I knew I needed to trust God and lean into the passions and strengths he had given me. But it was hard. It was a massive step of faith. I called my manager and asked her to meet me at a

Starbucks. Part of our discussion was supposed to be about my future with the company. Instead, I handed her my resignation. I almost vomited hearing the words come out of my mouth. After five years with a Fortune 500 company, I was walking away for a new career with no guarantees and no promises. I take that back. The guarantee I had was that God would provide. The promise I clung to was that he had a plan for my life. I just had to surrender to it. Thankfully, I did.

Looking back, it was one of the greatest decisions I ever made. Since that time I've enjoyed my work, been 100 percent fulfilled, and provided financially for my family. My new occupation is not really work. It's a ministry. It's God's business, not mine. Every day I thank him for the opportunity to help some wonderful people make important decisions that have a tremendous impact on their life. I just surrender to what he has for me each day and try to use my platform to be a blessing. Let me encourage you to trust God and surrender your work to him. It may require you to make some changes. But if God calls you to it, he will see you through it. He is good!

There is a very real challenge almost every person (and especially married couples) will face at some point. The challenge is this: How do we balance work and family? What happens when work and family collide? This is a tough one. As someone who is wired to achieve and be productive, I understand the challenge of flipping the switch and being a family man. It's tough, but it is possible. And winning here is so important to the well-being of our families.

Before I address this, let me say one thing: working hard and providing for your family are honorable things. There is nothing wrong with leaving the cave, killing something, and dragging it home. As previously mentioned, we were created for this. We just have to be careful about spending too much time out on the hunt away from the ones who will benefit from the hunt. To win in this area, we must be intentional. We must recognize that our to-do list will never completely go away. As I read one time, "When you die your inbox will still be full." Setting guardrails on time at the office, business travel, and computer use at home will help. Our families should be our top priority (outside of our relationship with God). Don't sacrifice precious moments with your family for one more client, paycheck, email, or phone call. Part of stewarding work well is keeping it in its proper place. Make it a matter of prayer and priority, and God will help you win this battle. When your life is nearing its end, you will remember those moments with your family. Chances are you will have forgotten those late nights at the office.

I also want to address this topic specifically from the viewpoint of a young family who desires for Mom to stay at home. Full disclosure here: I was raised by a stay-at-home mom and my wife currently stays at home with our boys. Yes, I may be a little biased. But, having talked to many people about this and having seen it play out time and time again, I feel very strongly about what I am going to say next. There is no greater calling for a young lady than to be a mother to her children. Period. Our culture is doing its best to brainwash us all into thinking a woman has no value if she doesn't go out into the marketplace and earn a paycheck. Nothing could be further from the truth.

God blessed females with a caring, nurturing quality that is uniquely given for the purpose of being a mom. What happens when a young child gets hurt? They want Mommy! What happens when little Johnny comes in hungry? "Mommy, fix me something to eat!" The bond between a mom and her children is special. Therefore, if you (ladies) feel called to come home and take care of your family, do whatever it takes to make this happen. Sell the car. Downsize the house. Skip a few trips to McDonald's. You will never regret spending quality time with your children as they are growing up. Any sacrifice you make in the workforce for the sake of your kids will be more than offset by the rewards of being a full-time mom. Do everything you can to be there for those precious moments.

I know there are mothers who would like to be at home more but can't be due to circumstances beyond their control. I also acknowledge that there are mothers who feel called to the workforce and find significance in gainful employment. If this describes you, I am certainly not trying to make you feel guilty. Just prayerfully consider how you can balance these very important roles in your life. When something must be sacrificed, do your best to not let it be quality time with your family. If you feel God tugging at your heartstrings about making a change, I encourage you not to ignore him.

Men, support your wives in this if they feel called to come home. Don't let money be the determining factor in this decision. I would argue that the value my wife currently brings to our household is far greater than any money she could earn in the marketplace. To take it a step further, her role is probably more important than my role as the breadwinner. Young families, make this a matter of prayer. What is God calling you to do? Surrender and you will be blessed.

The work we are called to, whatever that may be, is another stewardship opportunity. God blesses us with gainful employment to provide for our families. Whether you are a teacher, lawyer, policeman, or plumber, there is a work that is entrusted to you. Doing it to the best of your ability can be an act of worship. Many times we get bored in our jobs. We sometimes think the grass is greener on the other side. Be faithful in the task before you. When you steward it well, God will lead you where he wants you to go. On the other side of that coin is the temptation to become arrogant about our position or income. Never forget our energy, our minds, our income, and all opportunities are gifts from God. Deuteronomy 8:18 tells us, "But remember the Lord your God, for it is he who gives you the ability to produce wealth." We are simply called to manage each opportunity to the best of our abilities.

Before we conclude, there are some myths about work that I would like to dispel.

Myth #1: Work is a curse and is meant for punishment.

Work is not a curse from God. Yes, Adam sinned, and God said, "Cursed is the ground because of you. Through painful toil, you will eat food from it." However, if you study this passage closely, you will find work is actually ordained by God. Listen to the words of Tim Keller in his book *Every Good Endeavour*. "We are given specific work to do because we are made in God's image." He goes on to say, "Work has dignity because it is something that God Himself does and we do it in His place—as His representatives."[3] To subscribe to the thinking that work is a necessary evil is to say that work is only good when money is the end result. This means there is no other meaning in our work. That is simply not true.

God placed Adam and Eve in the garden to work it *before* the Fall occurred. Additionally, God worked. He created everything in six days and rested on the seventh day. Genesis 2:2: "By the seventh day God had finished the work He had been doing; so, on the seventh day, He rested from all His work." Therefore, work was around even before man was created.

Myth #2: The only reason we should work is to provide for our families.

Most of us go to work because we have bills to pay and family members we need to provide for. However, work is so much

---

3 Timothy Keller, *Every Good Endeavor* (New York, New York: Dutton Publishing, 2012).

more than just a means to our financial ends. God created us to work. Genesis 1:28 tells us, "God blessed Adam and Eve and said to them, "Be fruitful and increase in number. Fill the earth and *subdue* it." Genesis 2:5–15 tell us, "there was no man to work the ground...He took the man and put him in the garden to *work it* and take care of it." Work can be fulfilling, purposeful, and even enjoyable when surrendered to the Lord. Ephesians 2:10 tells us God prepared work for us to do: "We are God's *workmanship* created in Christ Jesus to do *good works* which God *prepared in advance* for us to do." There is great honor in the daily labor of the work God created specifically for us.

Myth #3: Our work defines us.

One of the first things we ask someone we are meeting for the first time is "What type of work do you do?" or "What do you do for a living?" I'm afraid many times we judge people based on their response. "I'm a doctor." Oh, he must make a lot of money. "I work on a construction crew." Oh, he must not have a college degree. "I'm in sales." Oh, I better end this conversation now! It is wrong for us to judge someone in this manner. Also, by doing so, we are affirming the false belief that this person's identity is wrapped up in their occupation. Nothing could be further from the truth.

In a previous chapter, I covered who we are in Christ. It has nothing to do with our job title. God can use a doctor, lawyer, plumber, teacher, sales representative, or any other occupation to accomplish his purposes. Yes, God was pleased with his work: Genesis 1:25 says, "And God saw that it was good." And yes, God wants our best at work: Colossians 3:23–24 says, "Whatever you do, work at it with all your heart, as working for the Lord, and not for men. Since you know that you will receive an inheritance from the Lord as a reward. It is the Lord Christ you are serving." But we should never allow our work to define us. It is the platform we, as children of God, have been given by him to impact his kingdom.

Surrendering to WIN

Myth #4: To rest from our work shows laziness.

Rest is also part of God's plan. He rested on the seventh day. We must guard against burning ourselves out by working too much. Without rest, we will struggle balancing all the other demands of life. Rest gives us time to reflect and recharge. If we never take a break from our work, three things happen:

1) Our quality of work begins to suffer.
2) Other priorities (like our families) are neglected.
3) Joy and fulfillment become more and more elusive.

Slowing down isn't a sign of laziness. It shows maturity and wisdom. Do not give in to the world's demands to put more on your plate than you can handle. God does not want us to operate outside of the capacity he gave us. To do so would be outside of his will for our lives.

Myth #5: Work and God should be kept separate.

As our country drifts further and further from God, more and more companies are asking Christians to leave God outside the building. In the name of not offending anyone, we are asked to not pray or talk about God while working. Let me be blunt: I refuse to work in an environment where God isn't welcome. If Christ truly lives inside of you, you can't help but take him to work with you. If he reigns supreme in your heart, you can't help but talk about him every day. I'm not trying to be ugly here, but if your employer is anti-God you need to be "anti-working there." On the contrary, work can be a great ministry. You do not have to work at a church or be in occupational ministry to be used by God. There really should be no separation of the sacred and the secular. Here are some practical ways you can use your work as ministry and as an act of worship:

- Do a great job. Be honest, work hard, and work with excellence.

- Be an example and witness to coworkers and business associates. Share the Gospel and your testimony when possible.
- Make as much money as you can so you can bless others. You can't give what you do not have.
- Use the skills and passions he gave you for his glory. Whatever you do, do it for the glory of God.
- Help people. Serve people. Love people. Let your words encourage and lift others up.

We are each unique and have different skill sets and passions. At the intersection of your passions (things you enjoy) and your skills (things you are good at) is a calling for you. Surrender to it and wholeheartedly pursue it. This provides you with the greatest opportunity to win in the workplace. No matter how old you are, it's never too late. Colonial Sanders didn't sell his first piece of chicken until he was in his sixties! At the time of this writing, my brother Michael is in medical school. He is forty-three years old and has five kids under the age of eight! Prayerfully consider what God is calling you to do (and pray for Michael!).

Here are a few questions to ask yourself:

1) Do I really enjoy what I currently do for a living?
2) Does my current occupation allow me to fully utilize the unique gifts and skills God gave me?
3) If money was not an issue, yet I still was required to work, what type of work would I do?

Think about your answers to those questions. Then surrender your answers to God, and allow him to move you to the vocation/calling he has for you. As they say, if you find something you enjoy doing, you will never have to work another day in your life.

Amen. Work is good. Work is available. Work gives our lives purpose and gives us a platform for ministry. Let's work as though we are working for the Lord and not for men. And when we do this, there is one direct benefit of our hard work we can't ignore. A paycheck. Money is the tangible result of hard work. In this next section, we will discuss being a good manager of our finances.

Simple Summary

1) Most people do not enjoy what they do for a living.

2) Attaining work-family balance is difficult but possible.

3) Work was created by God and is not a "necessary evil."

4) Our workplace can be our mission field.

5) When we use our gifts in the workplace for God's glory, work becomes an act of worship.

Section 3:
Our Treasures

Chapter 8

MANAGING GOD'S MONEY

Command those who are rich in this present world not to be arrogant nor to put their hope in wealth, which is so uncertain, but to put their hope in God, who richly provides us with everything for our enjoyment.

—1 Timothy 6:17–19

Stewardship and surrender are impossible to talk about without mentioning this next big topic. It's the area of our lives that we like to keep to ourselves and maintain control over. It's the elephant in the room that we try to hide from God and others. Yes, it's our money. Until now, this message of surrender and stewardship may have really resonated with you. "I'm a great manager of my time" or "I really think I use my talents every day!" are phrases that we might use when confronted with these biblical truths. How about our money? Ouch! That one hits us where it hurts.

We think it is ok to hold on tight to this area of our lives because "we work hard for our paychecks." I'm sure that's true. As a matter of fact, most people have no problem with a hard day's work. Leaving the cave, killing something, and dragging it home is the American way. But when that money hits our bank accounts, we become very possessive. We can say God owns it all as much as we want to, but our actions suggest that we believe our money is off limits to everyone but us. Managing debt, saving, giving, investing, budgeting, and spending are all key components of biblical financial stewardship. So how are we doing in these areas? The following statistics speak for themselves:

- According to Dave Ramsey, money problems are one of the leading causes of marital disagreements and the second leading cause of divorce.[1]
- According to TheBalance.com, Americans ended 2019 with $4.2 trillion in non-housing debt. Over $1 trillion of this debt came from credit cards. The average credit card balance for each person in the United States was $6,194.[2]
- According to *Time* magazine, student loan debt now totals over $1.5 trillion. The average borrower owes $30,000.[3]
- According to CNBC, 45 percent of baby boomers do not have any money saved for retirement.[4]
- According to Dave Ramsey, 78 percent of Americans live paycheck to paycheck.[5]
- GOBankingRates conducted a study that showed 69 percent of Americans have less than $1,000 in savings.[6]

---

1 Dave Ramsey, "Money Ruining Marriages in America" (daveramsey.com, February 7, 2018).
2 Kimberly Amadeo, "Is Your Credit Card Debt Higher than Average?" (thebalance.com February 13, 2020).
3 John Thune, and Mark Warner, "Americans Are Drowning in $1.5 Trillion of Credit Card Debt. There's One Easy Way Congress Could Help" (time.com, August 27, 2019).
4 Bob Pisani, "Baby Boomers Face Retirement Crisis—Little Savings, High Health Costs and Unrealistic Expectations" (cnbc.com, April 9, 2019).
5 Dave Ramsey, "How to Stop Living Paycheck to Paycheck" (daveramsey.com).
6 Cameron Huddleston, "Survey: 69% of Americans Have Less Than $1,000 in Savings" (gobankingrates.com, December 16, 2019).

- According to data compiled by NonprofitSource.com, only 5 percent of American families tithe and 80 percent give away 2 percent or less of their income.[7]
- The same study showed the average gift by adults who attend US Protestant churches was $17 per week.
- Additionally, 37 percent of regular church attenders and evangelicals do not give any money to the church.

Here is the harsh truth: on the whole, we are not winning with money. We have too much debt, not enough savings, and no margin to be used by God in this area of our lives. Let's go back to the most basic truths about money. God owns it. He blesses me with it. I am to manage it in a way that pleases him. His instruction manual (the Bible) gives us over two thousand nuggets of wisdom on what this looks like. That's it! Sounds so simple, right? So why do we continue to do things our way and not God's way? I'm glad you asked. Based on what I have personally observed over the years as I have counseled people about their money, I would like to propose six answers to this question.

1. Discontentment

Discontentment is a chief enemy of biblical stewardship. Deep down in our troubled souls is a longing for something more. There is an emptiness we attempt to fill in a lot of different ways. Somewhere along the line, we have bought into the lie that a bigger house, nicer car, or bigger TV will make us happy. That's just not the case. We can only sleep under one roof at a time. We can only drive one vehicle at a time. We can only wear one suit of clothes at a time (well, I guess you could attempt to wear more than one, but that might be a little uncomfortable!). Sooner or later (usually sooner), our new "toy" will become old and we will begin a search for the next latest and greatest. This is called discontentment.

---

[7] Nonprofit Source, *Charitable Giving Statistics* (nonprofitsource.com).

Surrendering to WIN

Hebrews 13:5 tells us to "keep your lives free from the love of money and be content with what you have." Listen again to those last six words: "be content with what you have." Here is something we must understand. God has promised to provide for us. He will meet our basic needs if we just trust him. I'm afraid we've really jacked this promise up by expecting him to give us everything we want! Listen to 1 Timothy 6:6–10 from the Message: "Be content with what God is doing in your life. Money doesn't bring happiness. Pursuing riches can lead to ruin and destruction."

In 2008 I went to Honduras on my first mission trip. While building a house there, I fell in love with two Honduran children. Keylin, a little girl who was nine years old at the time, and Jose, her six-year-old brother. At the end of the week, I knelt down beside them and through a translator asked what I could bring them from the United States when I returned the next year. I was thinking water guns, footballs, and Legos. With tears in their eyes, they both said the same two words at the exact same time: "*ropa y zapatos.*" Not knowing what this meant, I looked up at our translator. He smiled and said, "clothes and shoes." In that moment my heart was broken, but I also learned a valuable lesson on contentment. I had *wants* in mind for them. They had specific *needs* they knew had to be met. And, boy, did we meet them! The following year, we brought several bags of shoes and clothes. Jose and Keylin helped me understand what it meant to be content and trust God to meet my needs.

Let's go back to that deep emptiness we sometimes try to fill with stuff. That, my friends, is a God-shaped hole. More of *him* is what we need. He alone is the source of all satisfaction, contentment, and fulfillment. I have eaten great meals, won sports championships, ridden massive roller coasters, skied down huge mountains, participated in competitions with large crowds cheering, bought brand-new vehicles, sailed on giant cruise ships, walked down beautiful beaches, and experienced many other incredible things in my lifetime. None of these experiences provided lasting happiness. We can chase other things all we want and never be fully satisfied. Focus on Him. Christ is enough. We should never spend money in an attempt to satisfy our discontentment. Like the apostle Paul, we must learn to be content whatever our circumstances.

2. *Comparison*

Discontentment's first cousin is something known as the comparison trap. Why do we become so discontent? Because we compare ourselves to other people. Think about it this way. You have just bought a brand-new truck. For years you've had your eyes on a new Ford F-150 and you finally find the one. As you proudly drive it down the highway, another F-150 pulls up beside you. Yours is an XLT. The one beside you is a mac daddy King Ranch. Yours is a two-wheel drive. The King Ranch is a four-wheel drive. Yours has vinyl seats. Your new friend beside you has leather seats. All of a sudden, your excitement starts to diminish. *Why didn't I just go ahead and splurge for the King Ranch?* you ask yourself. *If I had bought the King Ranch, my friends would have been so impressed.* Five minutes earlier you were thrilled to have a new truck. Now you aren't sure you made the right decision. What changed? You compared your new purchase to someone or something else. You fell victim to the comparison trap.

The same can be said when you buy a new home. You love your new house, yard, kitchen, floor plan, and flooring. It is your dream home! God has blessed you so much in enabling you to raise your family in such a nice home. Until you get a chance to go visit your best friend's new home. Wow! This is really nice! A hint of jealousy creeps in. Then thoughts of making a few "upgrades" to your home fill your brain. Discontentment. Brought on by comparing. It's a trap. As financial guru Ron Blue often says, "I didn't know what I needed until I went to the mall!" So true. Be careful not to spend money just to keep up with the Smiths and the Joneses. By the way, the Smiths and Joneses are probably broke.

3. Selfishness

My little twin boys get along great. They love each other and play well together. Until there is a toy they both want. "I want it!" "I had it first!" "Give it to me!" "But it's mine!" Selfishness. Unfortunately, we are born with it, and our parenting styles only make it worse. We give our kids everything they need and most of the things they want. We are like Santa Claus 365 days a year! And then we expect them to be unselfish when they grow older. It just doesn't happen.

Our selfishness causes us to make decision after decision with one person and one thing in mind—me and my happiness. This is very unhealthy and eventually leads to financial difficulty. As Dave Ramsey says, "We buy things we don't need with money we don't have to impress people we don't like." To win with money, we must become more unselfish. We must allow God's resources to flow through us to bless others. More on this later. For now, just beware of selfish spending.

4. Confusion of Ownership

It's easy to say God owns it all. This is the heart of stewardship. He owns it. I manage it. We have a great partnership. However, saying it and living it are two different things. Most financial decisions are made through a "me" lens not a "he" lens. I have spoken to many groups of people about this topic. I always get a few head nods but a lot of blank stares when I say that he is the owner and we are managers. Let me make a bold statement. If God's people would embrace this one aspect of their Christian faith, it would change the world! I believe social injustices would be solved, lost souls would be saved, and the great commission would be fulfilled. Why do I feel so strongly about this? Because there are enough resources in this world to feed, clothe, and take care of all seven billion people. It is time for all Christ-followers to truly become his hands and feet. Because of our wealth, we have a greater opportunity to impact the world than any other generation. God has entrusted us with an abundance of blessing. Unfortunately, we have decided it was all for us and managed it poorly. We need to wake up and begin using God's resources to advance his kingdom.

5. Pride

Pride creeps into our personal finances in a number of ways. First of all, we rarely talk with anyone (even a financial professional) about our money. We do not want people to know how much money we make, how much money we have, and how much money we owe. Our culture has trained us (incorrectly) to judge each other on these numbers, so we keep them to ourselves at all costs.

Second, pride makes us think we can do this our way and not God's way. Saving, giving, paying down debt, and creating margin in our budgets goes against what we want to do with "our" money. So we stubbornly continue down the path we feel is best even if it goes against God's word.

Lastly, pride causes us to make bad decisions at times. This goes back to points one and two. We buy things we shouldn't buy or do things we shouldn't do because we do not want to be different than those around us.

6. Lack of Education

I heard a fellow say one time, "When I graduated high school, I couldn't create a budget, I couldn't balance a checkbook, and I didn't understand taxes, but I am so thankful I had the Pythagorean Theorem memorized!" Of course, he was joking, but this highlights a great point. For many years, good personal finance courses were missing in our school systems. This has gotten a little better in the last ten years, but there is still plenty of room for improvement.

And what about our churches? As previously mentioned, God's word is chock-full of financial wisdom. Why isn't this being taught more by the American church? Ron Blue has long argued that the church should be on the forefront of helping people win in the area of biblical stewardship. And it is not for a lack of material. Organizations like Ramsey Solutions, Crown Financial Ministries, and others have an abundance of great material just waiting to be utilized. I believe every church should have a team of people in place to help educate their members and teach them biblical financial principles. It needs to be a priority in our churches if we expect it to be a priority in other places.

I want to offer some wisdom from God's word that speaks to very specific aspects of personal finance.

What does the Bible say about debt?

- Proverbs 22:7: "The rich rule over the poor and the borrower is servant [slave] to the lender." Anyone who has ever found themselves drowning in debt can attest to this verse. The lender controls the borrower until the debt is paid back.
- Proverbs 22:26–27: "Do not be one who shakes hands in pledge or puts up security for debts; if you lack the means to pay, your very bed will be snatched from under you." I call this the repossession verse. If you have a loan against an asset, you technically do not own it. The lender can take it back at any time if payments are missed.
- Here is the bottom line when it comes to debt. The Bible doesn't say debt is a sin. However, it does warn us about the dangers of debt. It can negatively impact marriages, jobs, and many other aspects of a person's life. When you use consumer debt (credit cards, car loans, etc.), you are essentially stealing a lifestyle that you can't afford. Be very careful.

- God's word even speaks specifically about cosigning on a loan for a friend or family member. Proverbs 17:18: "One who has no sense shakes hands in pledge and puts up security for a neighbor." Translation: Don't do it!

Is saving money biblical or does it show a lack of faith?

- Proverbs 21:20: "In the house of the wise are stores of choice food and oil, but a foolish man devours all he has." There is wisdom in having financial margin. Inevitably, things will tear up, break down, and need repairing. Jobs will be lost, and unexpected expenses will pop up. Saving for a rainy day (three to six months of living expenses) is a good stewardship principle. Other things we should save for are down payments for new homes and big-ticket items like cars, appliances, and the like.
- Proverbs 6:6–11: "Go to the ant, you sluggard; consider its ways and be wise! It has no commander, no overseer or ruler. Yet it stores its provisions in summer and gathers its food at harvest. How long will you lie there, you sluggard? When will you get up from your sleep? A little sleep, a little slumber, a little folding of the hands to rest and poverty will come on you like a thief and scarcity like an armed man." There is an old saying: "Make hay while the sun is shining." The sun will not always shine. There is a time for saving up and time to lean on what has been saved.

What does the Bible say about giving?

- We serve a giving God. For God so loved the world, he *gave*. We cannot out-give God! Giving also breaks the power of money in our lives. More on this in the next chapter.

Surrendering to WIN

Does the Bible mention budgeting or spending?

- Luke 14:28: "Suppose one of you wants to build a tower. Will he not first sit down and estimate the cost to see if he has enough money to complete it?" We should sit down at the beginning of each month and "count the cost of our tower." We give every dollar a name. As Andy Stanley often says, "You gotta be knowing where your money is going!" There are many great ways to do this, including new apps available at no cost. We must have a plan for our money. Otherwise, it will disappear quickly, and we will never get ahead.

Does the Bible offer any investment advice?

- The greatest use of our money is to invest it in kingdom purposes. We will cover this in detail in chapter 9.
- While God doesn't tell us which stock, mutual fund, or asset class to invest in, he does offer some practical investing advice. Proverbs 13:11: "Dishonest money dwindles away, but whoever gathers money little by little makes it grow." Ecclesiastes 11:2: "Invest in seven ventures, yes, in eight; you do not know what disaster may come upon the land."
- God wants us to grow our money over time and diversify to avoid disaster.

Interestingly enough, there is one financial concept we speak of regularly that isn't even mentioned in the Bible—retirement. My mentioning of this might surprise you since I am a financial advisor. Do I think retirement is biblical? A recent newsletter I wrote for my clients will answer that question for you:

> Retirement! The mere sound of that word gets most of us excited. It's also a huge part of the American dream. We are taught to work hard, save money, and retire with a

large enough nest egg to kick back and enjoy life. Sounds great, doesn't it? But what does God's word say about retirement? Are you ready for this? Nothing. The word retirement cannot be found anywhere in the Bible. Nor do we find any examples of men and women shutting things down and taking life easy.

Does hearing these words take the wind out of your sails? Keep reading. You may also find it a bit odd hearing this news from a group of financial advisors. We think you will actually be encouraged (and hopefully inspired!) by what is said here. Let's consider a different view of "retirement" that is exciting and opens the door to so many incredible opportunities.

Instead of striving for retirement, consider another possible outcome of faithful financial stewardship. By making good financial decisions over extended periods of time, many people gain control over two of their most valuable assets—their time and their talents. Time that was spent punching a clock is now available to be used to pursue other passions. Talents that were possibly buried during the daily grind can now be resurrected and used for productive purposes.

We are all created in the image of almighty God. We are "fearfully and wonderfully" made and are set here on earth for a specific purpose. That purpose isn't designed to end at age sixty-five. Or seventy. Or any other age for that matter. As long as God sees fit to leave us here, we each have work to do. If our health allows, some of our most productive years very well could be those years *after* we free ourselves from the daily demands of a j-o-b.

That is not to say that someone should quit their current job the minute they no longer need a paycheck to make ends meet. Some may choose to continue earning an income for the sake of giving more away. Others may be thriving in their current position and have no desire to give it up. It is the responsibility of each of us to wrestle with what it is that God would have us do.

In closing, I want to challenge you to ask yourself a few questions:

1) Do I have an unhealthy obsession with retiring to a life of leisure? Is there some way I can use my time now to begin serving others and making a difference?
2) What are some of the God-given strengths that my career really has not allowed me to use? Is there a way I could turn those talents into a ministry that blesses others?
3) Are my finances currently holding me back from being all God created me to be? Am I so focused on the destination that I am not enjoying the journey?

John Piper tells the story of a married couple that worked thirty years in corporate America, retired at the age of fifty-two, and moved to Florida. For the rest of their lives, they "walked the beach and collected seashells." Piper poses the question, "When they stand before the good Lord one day, do you think He is going to want to see their seashell collection?"

The word retirement may not be in the Bible. But loving and serving people definitely is biblical. Be intentional about how you spend these precious years of your life. Joy, fulfillment, and blessings await you.

I cannot conclude this chapter on biblical financial stewardship without offering some practical advice. Here are some basic principles that hopefully will help you win in this area of life:

1) Have an emergency fund. Three to six months of living expenses should be set aside (not invested) in case you face unexpected financial difficulties.
2) Only consider fifteen-year fixed rate mortgages. While thirty-year mortgages are the most popular form of home debt, the extra interest paid over time is mind-boggling. Not to mention, you can be free and clear of a mortgage payment in half the time by financing for only fifteen years.
3) Spend less than you make. This starts with living on a budget. A budget is simply a spending plan that tells your money how to behave. Creating margin in your finances is critical to having financial peace.
4) Start early planning for college and retirement. Taking advantage of the time-value of money is critical to achieving financial goals. Do not procrastinate. There are many great savings vehicles available, but the key is to start early and take advantage of compounding interest.
5) Work toward becoming debt-free. This is a foreign concept in America today. Debt is readily available and considered normal. Most families have no idea how much additional pressure and stress they have because of debt payments. Have a plan to get out of debt. I highly recommend Dave Ramsey's "Financial Peace" class and *Total Money Makeover* book.

In Matthew 6:24, Jesus had this to say to his disciples: "No one can serve two masters. Either you will hate the one and love the other or you will be devoted to one and despise the other. *You cannot serve both God and money.*" He didn't say you cannot serve me and the devil. He didn't say you cannot serve me and your job. He specifically used the word "money." Over two thousand years ago, Jesus knew how important money would still be to us today. That's amazing! He knew then that money had the potential to compete with him for the thrones of our hearts. This, my friends, is a daily battle we all must fight. And we also must win! If we don't win this battle over the almighty dollar's grip on our lives, then Jesus will not (cannot) have his rightful place in our lives and hearts. Thankfully, he gives us all we need in his word to get the job done. Money isn't inherently evil. The love of money is the root of all kinds of evil. Money can be a great tool in the hands of a surrendered Christ-follower. It can make an eternal difference when managed God's way. This is the essence of stewardship: God's people using God's money to serve God's purposes for God's glory. Oh, may we view our money this way. If every professing follower of Jesus took financial stewardship seriously, the great commission would be funded, and the church would change the world.

Simple Summary

1) Managing money is one of the greatest stewardship responsibilities God gives us.

2) Statistics suggest we aren't doing a good job following biblical principles when it comes to personal finance.

3) We become discontent when we compare ourselves to others.

4) The Bible is full of wisdom on how we should manage God's money.

5) When we surrender our hearts to Jesus, money becomes a tool instead of a god.

Chapter 9

RADICAL GENEROSITY

*Each of you should give what you have decided
in your heart to give, not reluctantly or under compulsion,
for God loves a cheerful giver.*
—2 Corinthians 9:7

"For God so loved the world that He gave His one and only Son, that whoever believes in Him shall not perish but have eternal life." It is probably the world's best-known Bible verse. It is the salvation verse for any nonbeliever. It is a beautiful summary of the Christian faith. People even hold up signs at ball games displaying John 3:16. I have heard hundreds of sermons preached on this verse in my lifetime. But a few years ago, I recognized something that smacked me right between the eyes. God *gave*. We serve a giving God! He not only gave, but the gift he gave was his only son. I cannot fathom that level of giving. I have two sons, and I'm just not ready to give them up to be put to death—for anybody or anything! What my simple mind can comprehend is this: when I give, it makes me more like God. He gave his son. When I give, it also makes me more like Jesus. He gave his life. When we surrender our money to the Lord, giving should be a natural response. Let's explore what this looks like.

Giving should come much easier to us than it actually does. As Billy Graham used to say, "God has given us two hands—one to receive with and the other to give with. We are not cisterns made for hoarding; we are channels made for giving." Our Creator is the greatest giver of all time. In addition to the great gift of his son, God blesses us in so many other ways. He gives us life. He gives us health. He gives us wealth. He gives us relationships. He gives us abilities. He gives us pleasure. Everything we are and everything we have is a gift from him.

James 1:17 tells us, "Every good and perfect gift is from above, coming down from the Father of the Heavenly lights." If (and this is a big if) our lives are fully surrendered to God, giving should be easy and fulfilling. If in our heart of hearts we really believe that God is the creator and owner of all things and everything is a blessing from him, why would we not want to give? It goes back to Stewardship 101. I am not the owner. I am the manager of what he has entrusted to me. He asks me to give. He asks me to help meet needs around me. And yes, he even asks me to tithe (more on this later). I posed the question earlier: "Why would we not want to give?" Let's first answer the question "Why would we want to give?" By answering this question, I think the other question will answer itself.

So what would possess a person to take their hard-earned money and hand it over to someone or something else? Here are five reasons:

1) **To be obedient**. God's word calls for us to give. Malachi 3:10 says we are to give to the church: "Bring the whole tithe into the storehouse that there may be food in my house." James 2:15–16 says we should give to the needy: "Suppose a brother or a sister is without clothes and daily food. If one of you says to them, 'Go in peace; keep warm and well fed,' but does nothing about their physical needs, what good is it?" Luke 6:30 says we are to give to those who ask: "Give to everyone who asks you, and if anyone takes what belongs

RADICAL GENEROSITY

to you, do not demand it back." The Bible also tells us God loves a cheerful giver. We should give out of obedience.

2) **To show gratefulness for Christ's extravagant love for us.** I just mentioned God's generous gift to us. He gave us his son, and Jesus gave his life for us. We have been blessed far beyond what we each deserve. Out of the overflow of the blessings given to us should come a generosity to God and others. When we recognize God's rich blessing in our lives, it should prompt us to want to give.

3) **To break the power of money in our lives.** According to Matthew 6:24, we cannot serve both God and money. We must make a choice each day as to which we will give our hearts to. Having open hands and letting God's blessings flow through us is a great way to win that daily battle. And giving is actually fun! Being kind and generous to another person is one of the more fulfilling things we can ever do.

4) **To invest in God's kingdom.** One of my favorite books written on this topic is Randy Alcorn's *Treasure Principle*. Alcorn's famous line is "You can't take it with you, but you can send it on ahead!" When we direct the resources God has entrusted to us toward his kingdom work on this earth, the Bible promises certain rewards. One such reward for our "good deeds" here on this earth is treasures in heaven. Matthew 6:20–21 says, "But store up for yourselves treasures in heaven, where moths and vermin do not destroy, and where thieves do not break in and steal. For where your treasure is, there your heart will be also." This is an amazing truth! We have the opportunity to trade in our temporary currency (money) for a

currency (heavenly treasures) that will pay dividends forever. How do we do this? By making generous investments into God's economy. Kingdom investments have eternal rewards. If that doesn't motivate us to give, nothing will.

Here is a simple example of this powerful truth. A few months ago, our church took a mission team to Honduras. Before I left, a friend of mine approached me and handed me some Honduran lempira. He too had visited Honduras recently but had forgotten to exchange the lempira back to American dollars before he left. They were no good to him here. I could use them in the country I was headed to. I hope you are beginning to see the parallel. We obsess about our money as though we will be able to use it forever. Instead we should look at exchanging it for eternal treasures by investing in the kingdom of God.

Maybe this humorous story will further illustrate this powerful principle. A rich man died and went to heaven. He couldn't wait to see what his heavenly mansion looked like since he knew it would be even greater than his earthly mansion. Saint Peter met him at the entrance and began walking him toward his eternal destination. Sure enough, the homes were incredibly beautiful. As the rich man was anxiously anticipating the sight of his new home, he noticed a disturbing trend—the houses were getting smaller and smaller the farther they went. Eventually they arrived at a tiny house on a corner lot.

"Welcome to your new home!" Peter proclaimed.

"But I don't understand," said the rich man. "My home on Earth was bigger than this. I thought heaven would be so much better."

"Sorry to disappoint you," said Saint Pete. "But we did the best we could with the money you sent us ahead of time!"

Obviously, this is just a joke. We can't deposit actual currency in the Bank of Heaven and have it waiting on us when we arrive. However, the Bible speaks very clearly about storing up treasures in heaven. There is a clear biblical connection between our faithful stewardship of God's resources and the eternal rewards we will receive one day.

5) **To help those in need**. There are needs all around us. The Bible asks us to care for orphans, widows, our neighbor, the least of these, and anyone else he puts in our path. There is a beautiful example of this in the early Acts church. Those early believers were literally willing to sell their own possessions to help meet the needs of their fellow man. Listen to this verse in Proverbs 28:27: "Those who *give to the poor* will lack nothing, but those who close their eyes to them will have many curses." We are blessed when we help meet the needs of the poor. But we are cursed when we turn a blind eye.

As surrendered Christians, we should go through life with our head on a swivel looking for ways to use God's money to bless others. He also asks us to support his bride, the church, financially. This leads me to a somewhat controversial topic around the subject of giving: tithing.

Two men were stranded on a deserted island. One of them was worried and stressed while the other one continued to be relaxed. Finally the first one asked the man who didn't seem to be too worried, "Why aren't you concerned?"

The man replied, "Because I make one million dollars per year."

"What! The amount of money you make does you no good out here, right?"

"Oh, yes it does," the other man replied. "Because I also tithe. I promise my preacher will find me!"

What exactly does tithing mean? When we speak of tithing, we are usually referring to the practice of giving 10 percent of our income to the local church. But did you know in Old Testament times, most Israelites actually were commanded to give three different sums of money totaling almost 23 percent? There was a Levitical tithe, a festival offering, and a charity offering. Imagine what would happen if a 23 percent commitment were required today to join a Christian church. Sadly, I suspect the church would lose a lot of its members.

Those who argue against tithing will say things like "tithing is legalistic" or "tithing is no longer required because we are no longer under the old law." Those who argue for tithing are usually just upset at those who aren't tithing. Statistics suggest that a large number of people fall into the category of non-tithers. According to Nonprofits Source, somewhere between 10 and 25 percent of evangelical Christians actually give 10 percent of their income. On average, they give 2.5 percent instead of 10 percent or greater.[281] Before I address the two tithing concerns mentioned earlier, let me say this: whether you agree with tithing or not, these statistics are very concerning.

In a time of unparalleled prosperity and freedom, Christians are failing miserably in their mandate to help fund the great commission. We have chosen instead to live like kings, hoard our money, and invest in ourselves rather than God's kingdom. If every follower of Jesus simply committed to live on 90 percent (or less) of their income instead of 100 percent (or more, usually), the church could change the world! Needs would be met,

---

1 Nonprofit Source, *Charitable Giving Statistics* (nonprofitsource.com).

souls would be saved, and the Gospel would be spread to the ends of the earth. Missionaries would be funded, hungry children would be fed, and God's kingdom would grow exponentially. The church's reputation would change from an organization of rules to an organization of love. Christians would be praised instead of seen as hypocrites.

So do I believe in tithing? Yes! Do I believe in legalistically setting aside 10 percent of your income to earn the favor of God? No! I want to see changed hearts that are not asking the question "How much do I have to give?" but rather "What are the needs God has blessed me to be able to meet?" Let's get away from asking questions like "Before or after taxes?" and "If I give money to some other cause, is it ok for me to reduce the amount I give my church?" Those questions reveal a heart issue. "What is the least I can get away with giving and still please God?" does not flow from a surrendered heart that desires to be a good steward. The better question to ask is "What does God want me to do with his money?" I fully believe part of that answer is to support his bride, the church.

Think about it this way: I suspect most Christians would agree the church is the bride of Christ. What if you left town for an extended period and asked a trusted friend to take care of your spouse? You also provided the money to help meet his or her needs. Upon returning, you find out all the money was spent on your friend and not your spouse. Not a pretty picture, is it? Such is the case when we do not use God's money to take care of God's church. By the way, Dave Ramsey gives a great answer to the before or after taxes question: Do you want to be blessed on the gross or the net? I think I know the answer to that one.

That leads me to the other tithing argument. Wasn't the tithe just an Old Testament mandate that went away when Jesus issued in a new covenant? As we have already stated, tithing was instituted under the old Levitical law. Additionally, Jesus only mentioned tithing one time in the New Testament, in Matthew 23:23: "Woe to you, teachers of the law and Pharisees, you hypocrites! You give a tenth of your spices—mint, dill and cumin. But you have neglected the more important matters of the law—justice, mercy and faithfulness. You should have practiced the latter, without neglecting the former."

Those who argue tithing is no longer required will point to grace instead of the law and cheerful giving as a replacement to mandated percentage giving. Here is my question: "If tithing was required under the old law, do you think Jesus raised or lowered the standard when he came?" I think you know the answer, but if you don't, let's see what the scripture says. Under the old law, the commandment was to not kill. Under Jesus's new covenant, if you hate your brother, it's as though you have murdered him. Under the old law, the act of adultery was against the rules. Jesus said, "Anyone who looks at a woman lustfully has already committed adultery with her in his heart." It's pretty obvious Jesus didn't lower the bar. The standard was raised when Jesus issued in a new covenant.

Additionally, we actually see tithing modeled *before* Moses receives the law on Mount Sanai. In Genesis 14 Abram (later named Abraham) gives a tenth of all he had to King Melchizedek. This is the first example in scripture of a tithe being given. Another prelaw example can be found in Genesis 28:22. Jacob makes a vow to God to give him a tenth of all that God blesses to Jacob's care.

Pastor Robert Morris, in his best-selling book *The Blessed Life*, describes tithers and non-tithers. He says without exception he hears from the tithers, "I am so blessed. Or God has truly blessed me." The non-tithers typically say, "I can't afford to tithe."[2]

---

2 Robert Morris, *The Blessed Life* (Grand Rapids, Michigan: Bethany House Publishers, 2002).

Think about those statements, and let the truth of what's being said here sink in. If you are not tithing, you are missing out! You are missing out on pure joy. You are missing out on God's blessing in your life. And, as previously mentioned, you are missing out on eternal rewards. I would argue you can't afford *not to* tithe! Pastor Tony Evans describes the non-tithing church attenders as spiritual teenagers. They want to enjoy all the benefits of the home without helping pay the bills!

Giving 10 percent of pretax income to the church is the training wheels of giving. It isn't the finish line; it's the starting point. If we truly acknowledge our money is a gift from God and surrender our hearts completely to him, there will be other things God will ask us to do. In some churches, money given above the tithe is called an offering. Call it whatever you want, but I do not believe 10 percent is the stopping point. Here are a few examples of ways to invest in the kingdom above and beyond what you contribute to your church's operating budget.

- Supporting missionaries: There is no better way to put your money to work reaching lost people than supporting those who are on the front lines. Money invested here allows those who are called to the mission field to be free to share the Gospel and make the name of Jesus known daily in places you may never go.
- Less fortunate: In every city, state, and country, there are those who are struggling. Whether it's the poor, the widowed, or abandoned children, our money can make a huge difference in helping them. We are called to bear each other's burdens (Gal. 6:2). And here is some incredible news: Jesus said, "Whatever you did for one of the least of these brothers of mine, you did for Me." Helping the less fortunate equals helping Jesus.
- Social causes: I will use abortion as an example here. A problem like abortion seems too big for us to be

able to make a difference in. Donations to organizations who are in the fight against these sinful practices are a great way to make a kingdom impact. We only have one abortion clinic in my home state of Mississippi. Recently, a Center for Pregnancy Choices clinic opened up across the street from this clinic. Supporting ministries like this puts God's money to work directly against a sin that breaks his heart.

- Other church ministries: Most churches have numerous budget line items. Some of these are normal operating expenses (electricity, water, salaries, etc.), while others are more ministry related. Giving to the church's building fund, missions, or some other ministry of the church can be a great kingdom investment. Just yesterday I had a gentleman from another church come to my house to pick up some old furniture. He was organizing a large garage sale to raise funds for his church. I only spent a few minutes with Mr. Vernon, but I could see that his motives were pure and his heart was in the right place. I can't imagine God not honoring his efforts when he arrives at his eternal destination.
- Parachurch ministries: There are many great Christian nonprofit organizations making a difference in God's kingdom. Finding one whose values and mission statement line up with a cause near and dear to your heart should not be very hard. For me, it's a ministry called Expanding Borders. I know their leaders well and love the kingdom work they are doing in Honduras. It is easy for me to send money to Expanding Borders. Every dollar goes to helping orphaned children, educating the poor, and evangelizing the lost. I get excited seeing the kingdom impact of our contributions.

RADICAL GENEROSITY

- Short-term mission trips: At some point most of us will receive a letter from someone going on a short-term mission trip. The letter typically asks for prayer and money. Let me encourage you not to toss the letter in the wastebasket with no consideration of helping the sender. If someone is willing to take the Gospel to the ends of the earth, the least we can do is help ease the financial burden. If writing a check for $250 means someone in a third world country hears about Jesus, that is an incredible return on your investment! I love getting those letters. I hope by reading this you will begin to get excited about them too. Mission trips change lives. Both the person going and the people ministered to receive a blessing. We can also be blessed by simply offering financial support. It's a great kingdom investment that directly funds the great commission.

The church was established in the book of Acts. Listen to the way these new believers looked out for each other. Acts 2:44–45: "All the believers were together and had everything in common. They sold property and possessions to give to anyone who had need." This generosity continues in Acts 4:32–35 "All the believers were one in heart and mind. No one claimed that any of their possessions was their own, but they shared everything they had. With great power the apostles continued to testify to the resurrection of the Lord Jesus. And God's grace was so powerfully at work in them all that there were no needy persons among them. For from time to time those who owned land or houses sold them, brought the money from the sales and put it at the apostles' feet, and it was distributed to anyone who had need."

What could possibly prompt this level of generosity? Only a transformed heart. For these early Christ-followers, the old had been made new. The flesh had given way to the Holy Spirit to work in their lives. Oh, that we could experience transformation like this in today's church! We have been blessed beyond measure but have mismanaged God's money in so many ways. Let's turn our hearts back to almighty God and away from the almighty dollar. Let's be a people known for our giving and generosity. Let's surrender to biblical financial stewardship.

Scott Rodin recently wrote about what the heart of the faithful steward looks like. He said, "it means giving without being asked. It is selfless, demanding no repayment and expecting no return. It does not need to be motivated by any external inviting or human appeal. The love of a steward looks for ways to give, listens for God's voice for where and how much to give, and rests in the Holy Spirit that regardless of the sacrifice, God will always provide."[3]

As I conclude this chapter, don't miss this final truth: God doesn't need your money. That's right. All this talk on giving, and he doesn't even need your money. Want to know why? It all belongs to him anyway! What he wants from you is your heart! In Mark 10 we read about an encounter Jesus had with a rich young ruler. When asked what he needed to do to inherit eternal life, Jesus replied, "go sell everything you have, and give to the poor." Jesus didn't need the man's money. But this young leader had a heart issue. He walked away sad and grieved. His money and possessions were on the throne of his heart.

You see, when Jesus has our hearts, our money naturally flows into his kingdom work. When our hearts are 100 percent surrendered to him, biblical stewardship is the result. The reciprocal of that is also true. Our hearts follow where we invest our money. If you do not believe this, take all your money and purchase one company's stock shares with it. You will suddenly become much more interested in learning about that company, their earnings

---

3 Scott Rodin, *The Steward's Journey*. Good Friday. https://thestewards journey.com/good-friday/

projections, their product lines, and their business model. You will likely support the company, read articles about them, and perk up when their name is mentioned on television. Your heart has followed your treasure. That's why it is so important to place your treasures into God's kingdom. In the next chapter, I hope to give you one more compelling reason.

Simple Summary

1) We serve a giving God. When we give, we are more like him.

2) We should not only give out of obedience but also to break the power of money in our lives.

3) Tithing is a good starting point for any giving plan.

4) The early church paints a beautiful picture of generosity for us.

5) God doesn't need our money. He already owns it all! He wants our hearts.

Chapter 10

THE PROSPERITY OF THE GOSPEL

Give, and it will be given to you.
A good measure, pressed down,
shaken together and running over, will be poured
into your lap. For with the measure you use,
it will be measured to you.
—LUKE 6:38

I am fully aware I am taking a chance by writing this chapter. At the risk of sounding as though I'm promoting a prosperity gospel, I want to take a strong look at some of the biblical truths related to this topic. Time and time again, we see God honor obedience, surrender, and stewardship. I realize there are some churches and pastors across the country who present a feel-good version of the Gospel in the hopes of growing their congregation size and increasing revenue. This "follow Jesus, and you will receive financial gain" message isn't biblical and does more harm to the kingdom than good. So does the "name it and claim it" version of Christianity. So before I look at some of the Bible's promises about "prospering," let's first address five falsehoods prevalent today.

#1: If I give my life to Christ, everything is easy from that point forward.

Nowhere in scripture does it say being a Christian is easy. In fact, Jesus himself said quite the opposite. He said if we are to follow him, we must deny ourselves. Denying ourselves isn't exactly a picture of taking the easy road. He also said we must take up our cross daily. Taking up a cross in those days signified a brutal death. Nothing is easy about that! Being a Christian isn't easy. It is, however, worth it.

#2: If I give some money to the church, God will make me rich.

Let's be clear about two things. First, God doesn't need our money. He can accomplish whatever he wants whenever he wants without you, me, or any of our resources. Second, if your motive for giving is to receive something in return, you might as well keep your hard-earned money. God is way more interested in our hearts than in our wallets. We give to our church out of obedience and love for him. We give to help fund the ministries of the local church and to meet needs. We give because we know it belongs to him and we desire to invest it where he is working. God does not promise to double our assets if we drop a twenty-dollar bill in the offering plate each week.

#3: If I pray hard enough and just trust God, he will bless me with material success.

Bigger houses, fancy cars, and more money aren't what God meant when he promised to provide for us. Most of the time, our motives for wanting these things are selfish. God promises to feed us and clothe us. He knows our basic needs. Now, it is true that he is a loving Father and desires to bless us. However, his idea of blessing us may look very different from what we think it should look like.

#4: If I "delight myself in the Lord," he will give me whatever I want.

I have heard several people claim Psalm 37:4 as their life verse. "God promises to give me the desires of my heart," they say. Yes and no. Let me share with you what I have learned about that verse. When I truly "delight myself in the Lord," the desires of my heart change. For many years my heart's desire was business success and financial gain. When I truly surrendered my heart to him, those desires took a back seat to kingdom work. Point being, when we align our desires with his desires, he will absolutely give us what we want. Because what *we* want is now exactly what *he* wants. His plans, not our plans, are now the priority.

#5: If I become a Christian, nothing bad will ever happen to me or my family again.

To dispel this myth, we need not look any further than to other countries where our brothers and sisters in Christ are being persecuted for their faith. Joining the family of God means we are forgiven from sin, not protected from the sins of others. Jesus himself, the only perfect person, died a horrible death. So no, following him doesn't put life on cruise control. We live in a broken world. One day Jesus will come back and make all things right. Our hope is in the perfect, pain-free next life, not those qualities in this one.

So if these five things aren't true, what does the Bible say about God's people being blessed for their faithfulness and stewardship? Here are some verses that speak directly to this topic:

Malachi 3:10 says, " 'Bring the whole tithe into the storehouse, that there may be food in my house. Test me in this,' says the Lord Almighty, 'and see if I will not throw open the floodgates of heaven and pour out so much blessing that there will not be room enough to store it.' " This passage, written by the prophet

Malachi, was both a strong reminder and an encouragement to Israel. Malachi accuses Israel of "robbing God" by not giving their tithe. This is a unique passage of scripture, because in most cases "testing" or "tempting" God is discouraged. However, Malachi's word from the Lord literally challenges the descendants of Jacob to test God. The reward for their obedience was an uncontainable blessing. When we are faithful to give, God is faithful to pour out his blessings on us.

The passage in Matthew 25:14–30, known as the Parable of the Talents, tells the story of a master who left home and entrusted "talents," which represented sums of money, to his servants. They were to care for the property and manage it well while the master was away. Upon returning, the master found that two of them were faithful stewards. To them he said, "Well done good and faithful servants. You have been faithful with a few things. I will put you in charge of many things. Come and share your master's happiness." One servant did not manage the money well. He buried it and had nothing to show for it upon the master's return. To him the master said, "You wicked and lazy servant!" The money was taken from this servant and given to someone else.

The Parable of the Talents is rich with stewardship principles. Like this master, our Heavenly Father has gone away and entrusted his riches to us. He will return one day and judge us for how we managed his resources. Will we hear, "Well done, good and faithful servant," or will we be called "wicked and lazy," or possibly "greedy and selfish"? Either way, this passage speaks directly to rewards for faithful stewardship. When we are faithful in the small things, God blesses us with greater opportunities.

Luke 16:10–12 says that "Whoever can be trusted with very little can also be trusted with much, and whoever is dishonest with very little will also be dishonest with much. So if you have not been trustworthy in handling worldly wealth, who will trust you with true riches? And if you have not been trustworthy with someone else's property, who will give you property of your own?" This is very similar to the lesson of the last parable. Faithful stewardship, no matter how insignificant the task may seem, usually leads to greater responsibility.

Proverbs 11:24–25 says that "one person gives freely, yet gains even more; another withholds unduly, but comes to poverty. A generous person will prosper; whoever refreshes others will be refreshed." When we bless others, we in turn are also blessed. Generosity is fulfilling and rewarding. But many times, when we aren't willing to meet the needs of others, we find ourselves struggling as well. Again, there seems to be a powerful connection between faithful management of God's resources and the blessings we receive from God.

Luke 6:38 tells us, "Give, and it will be given to you. A good measure, pressed down, shaken together and running over, will be poured into your lap. For with the measure you use, it will be measured to you." I spent several hours researching exactly what Jesus meant in this passage. Pastor Tony Evans offered the best commentary. He describes what is taking place here as the Law of the Harvest. We receive what we are willing to give. Many times, we limit what flows *into* our lives because we do not let much flow *out of* our lives. We are blessed to be a blessing. And when we are a blessing, we keep getting blessed. It's a great cycle! We are more like pleasant streams than stagnant ponds. God's blessings must flow through us in order for us to be replenished. And this includes more than just our money. It applies to love, forgiveness, and grace as well. Listen to what Pastor Evans says in his book *Horizontal Jesus*:

> This principle helps explain why so many of us believers are not seeing more evidence of God showing up on every level of our lives. God doesn't appear to be showing

up experientially in our vertical relationship with Him because we are refusing to give practically in our horizontal relationship with others. The problem is we want God to meet our needs, but we're not willing to give to anyone else. A lot of Christians want to be blessed, but they do not want to give more of themselves—their time, talents, and treasures—to God for the benefit of others. They want their needs met in the *"pressed down shaken together"* way Jesus described in Luke 6:38 without fulfilling the principles and precepts of the *"one another"* passages of scripture. Being a conduit for blessing is critical to experiencing true blessing from God.

He goes on to explain (based on 1 Corinthians 2:9) six rules of the harvest:

1) Your harvest depends on whether you sow.
2) Your harvest depends on how you sow.
3) Your harvest depends on how much you sow.
4) Your harvest depends on where you sow.
5) Your harvest depends on when you sow.
6) Your harvest depends on why you sow.[1]

Let me say it one more time: we do not give to get. God does not promise to make us rich if we are generous. But we do live in a sowing and reaping world. And he teaches us in his word what biblical stewardship looks like and calls for us to be obedient. God owns everything under the sun. He entrusts his world to us. He tells us how to manage it. He wants to bless us when we are faithful and obedient.

Think about this "blessing" from a very practical perspective.

---

[1] Tony Evans, *Horizontal Jesus* (Eugene, Oregon: Harvest House Publishers, 2015).

THE PROSPERITY OF THE GOSPEL

If you were going out of town and asked another couple to house-sit for you, what would your expectations be? If upon returning the dog was dead because he had not been fed, two windows were knocked out from a party the couple threw, and there was mud all over the carpet, would you give them more responsibility? Would you trust them to babysit your kids? No! You probably would not even ask them to cut your grass in the future. They didn't take good care of your property. What if, on the other hand, they did a great job? You would bless them in some way. And likely trust them with greater responsibility. Such is the case with God as well.

What does all this mean? I wholeheartedly believe God rewards faithful stewardship. He examines our hearts and watches our actions every minute of every day. God truly wants to bless those who are fully committed to him. "For the eyes of the Lord move to and fro throughout the earth that he may strongly support those whose heart is completely His" (2 Chron. 16:9). Amen! I don't know about you, but I'm all for having the good Lord as my strong supporter. God loves us with a love so great our feeble minds cannot comprehend it. And just as we love our children and want things for them, he wants to bless his children as well. I would not say these things if I had not experienced this in my own life. Every time Aubrey and I have fully surrendered a decision, situation, or possession to God, he has done amazing things. He has done things only he can do. The following story illustrates one of God's greatest blessings in our lives. We surrendered to him, and he showed up in a mighty way.

In many ways this story begins over thirty-five years ago in a small North Mississippi town called Walnut. On July 2, 1982, Aubrey Brook Alexander (who is now my wife) was born to Ron and Vicki Alexander. Upon leaving the hospital, Ron and Vicki brought their beautiful blond-haired daughter home to 80 Bell Lane just outside of town. The reason the road was named Bell Lane is because just beyond the Alexander residence was the old

Bell home, located at 81 Bell Lane. This hundred-year-old home was occupied by Wallace and Joyce Bell, Aubrey's grandparents. Those details are important because the close proximity between these two homes laid the foundation for what became a grandmother-granddaughter relationship unlike any other. Aubrey was the apple of Joyce Bell's eye. Not only did she live fifty yards from her new granddaughter, but Aubrey was also Joyce's first grandchild. To say that she spoiled Aubrey would be the understatement of the century.

As the years passed and Aubrey grew up, Mrs. Joyce gradually moved from grandmother to mentor and then mentor to friend—best friend, might I add. She was always there to encourage, listen, or do whatever Aubrey needed her to do. They talked daily and visited each other often. Even after Aubrey was grown, Mrs. Joyce still wanted Aubrey to sit on her lap. She loved on Aubrey like she was still a small child. It was an incredible relationship based on unconditional love. On the morning of January 10, 2011, Aubrey and I were awakened by a phone call from Vicki, Aubrey's mother. Mrs. Joyce Bell had passed away suddenly at age seventy-two. She had an infection in her brain that had claimed her life on that cold winter morning. We immediately packed up and headed to Walnut to be with family and mourn the loss of a sweet, lovable, godly lady.

Aubrey's grandmother, mentor, and best friend had gone home to be with Jesus. It was a crushing time for Aubrey and her family. The life of the party was no longer at the party. The center of attention no longer needed any attention. The outgoing Christian lady whom everyone loved and adored had been taken from this earth prematurely. Her absence left a void that no one else could fill. We didn't understand it at the time. It just didn't make sense. Why did she have to die? How was this world better off without Joyce Bell in it? As long as we were "leaning on our own understanding," it didn't make sense. But the Bible tells us to trust in the Lord. So we did. And one year later, we would get our answer.

Before I fast-forward to January 10, 2012, allow me to share a few background details leading up to that day. After Aubrey and I had been married three or four years, we decided we were ready for children. For a number of reasons, we were unable to get pregnant. This went on for several years, until finally we began to look at other options. Foster care? Adoption? Should we just give up altogether on the idea of being parents? God began working on our hearts around the idea of international adoption. In the beginning, I was completely resistant. First of all, I just didn't really want to adopt. Second, if we did adopt, I wanted my child to look like me. I couldn't picture myself the father of a child from Africa, China, or even Honduras, the country where we did mission work. God used many people, songs, and sermons to reach our hearts. Finally, in 2010, we surrendered to God's call for us to adopt a child from Africa. The decision was difficult and was not even fully supported by some members of our own family. Never in our wildest dreams did we think we would one day consider adopting a child from another country. Yet we knew with 100 percent certainty God was calling us to do it. We surrendered and submitted our application. This began what we thought would be a two-to-three-year international adoption process.

Our application was finally approved in May 2011, so we mailed in our first check. This was on a Friday. The following Tuesday, Aubrey went back in to see her doctor. Her purpose for the visit was to go back on birth control. All God's Children, the adoption agency we were using, terminates anyone who gets pregnant during the adoption process. We wanted to fully focus on what God had told us to do. Instead, God blew our minds one more time! Aubrey found out that day she was pregnant. I was so stunned. It literally took her thirty minutes to convince me she was telling the truth. So, the following week, I went with her to our very first ultrasound appointment. In that dark little exam room, a friendly nurse began to show us the activity in Aubrey's belly.

"See that right there? You are definitely pregnant. That's a tiny heartbeat."

"Awe," we both exclaimed. "So cool!"

So this was God's plan all along. But God wasn't done surprising us.

"However," the nurse said.

Oh no! we thought. *"Howevers" are never good.*

"This baby has company!" said the nurse. "Do twins run in your family?"

Wow! Had God given us two for the price of one? Sure enough. We were not only pregnant, but Aubrey was also carrying two identical boys in her belly. God is good. Or is he? We soon found out it was a complicated pregnancy. Our doctor told us one of the boys would not make it. But our God had given us two, not one. So we prayed. And we trusted. And we continued to surrender. I cannot even begin to describe to you the peace we had during the entire pregnancy. God had led us to it, and we knew he would carry us through it. Those were his babies, not ours.

On the morning of January 10, 2012, twin boys Max and Miles Broome arrived. It was one year to the day of Joyce Bell passing away. Instead of a time of mourning for the loss of a loved one, it was a time of celebrating new life. Aubrey's mom was there. Aubrey's grandfather was there. It was a happy day. Yes, everyone longed for Joyce Bell to be there. But she was in heaven. Call me crazy, but I'm compelled to believe her first request in heaven was for God to answer Aubrey's prayer to become a mother. And now we were proud parents of not just one child but two. God is good! I really believe that call to adoption was an Abraham moment for us. We struggled with what we were being asked to do, but in the end we were obedient. And God showed up in a mighty way. It

THE PROSPERITY OF THE GOSPEL

has been my experience on more occasions than I could count that he takes over when we surrender to him.

"Yeah, but that has nothing to do with money, possessions, or prosperity," you may say. This next personal testimony of God's faithfulness is just for you. My personal experience suggests God also honors faithful stewardship. In 2014 a young couple from my church came into my office. They were struggling financially, and life had seemingly beat them down. It wasn't that their income was too low. They had a great income! The problem was some of the decisions they had made. After marriage they bought a new house on a thirty-year mortgage. Then they bought a new vehicle for him. Then one for her. Next thing you knew, they were drowning in debt and had very little margin in their budget. They came to me for help and advice.

Long story short, this couple took seriously the principles I laid out before them. They sold their house and moved back in with his parents. They sold one vehicle and carpooled to work. They began saving all of her paycheck each month. They built up a nice emergency fund and began saving for a down payment on their next home. After eighteen months, they were financially free again. A huge burden had been lifted off their shoulders. Life was so much better now. They bought their own home on a twenty-year note and put 10 percent down at closing. Their one vehicle was fully paid for. All they had left to do was save up for a second vehicle and they would be all set.

During the time I counseled them, God began tugging at my heart to help them in a big way. This was a couple that desired to do things the right way. They were a great family with two beautiful small children. They loved God and just wanted to do his will in their life. I began prayerfully considering how God would have me help them. I kept coming back to the same challenge from God: *give them your van*. What! My family needed our van. As previously mentioned, I had two small kids of my own. What would we drive? How would I buy another vehicle? I had not been planning to vehicle shop for another three to four years. But God's message rang through loud and clear. *Give them your van!*

During the time I was wrestling with this, I attended a conference in Dallas at Gateway Church. Pastor Robert Morris was speaking, and these were his words to our group: "When you start looking for a new vehicle, don't trade in or sell your old one. Find a couple who needs it and give it to them." He went on to say he had given away numerous vehicles over the years. Ok, God. I get it. I will obey you and trust you. So when I got home, my wife and I called this couple and asked them to meet us at the local ice cream shop. While sitting there talking to them, Chris Tomlin's hit song "How Great is Our God" came through the speakers. This was it. In that moment I needed to just tell them what God had told me. So I did. And they were speechless. And then tears were shed (some of them mine). I told them I had no idea what we were going to do but they would be getting our van as soon as I figured it out.

Within a few weeks, a great deal on a used van popped up at the local Honda dealership. It was exactly what we were looking for. Coincidence? I think not. After some negotiating, we drove away in a replacement van. We said our goodbyes to the old one and drove it back to the ice cream shop one final time. The young couple drove home that night in an answer to their prayers. They now had two vehicles and didn't have to go back into debt at all. We drove home with hearts grateful for God having allowed us to be able to bless them. Little did we know, the story was far from over.

A few weeks later, I received notice that the broker-dealer I'm affiliated with was giving us a lump sum of money. There was nothing we needed to do to receive this money, and we did not have to pay it back. It was simply a way for them to say thank you to us for sticking with them through some recent changes. My lump sum amount? You guessed it. I received more than enough to cover the costs of our new van. Have I mentioned that God is good? And that he provides? When we are obedient and surrender it all to him, he is faithful to meet our every need. And sometimes blow our minds! Please hear my heart in telling you these two stories. I am not bragging on Neal. I am bragging on God. He has proven himself faithful time and time again in my life. You cannot out-give God! Or, as Anne Frank stated, "No one has ever become poor by giving."

I'm sure you have some stories like this as well. Times when God did something incredible as a result of your obedience. There just seems to be a direct connection between faithful stewardship and God's rich blessings. Think back to the Gospel of Jesus Christ. There is prosperity in it. Jesus *gave* his life for us. We *receive* the benefits of his death on the cross. We are able to *prosper* because of what he did for us. A great inheritance awaits all of us who have given our lives to Christ.

Let me say this one final time. God doesn't promise to make us rich if we are generous. We can't just "name it and claim it." But he does bless us when we manage his resources according to his instructions. He tells us he has plans for us and they are good. His plans for us are to allow us to prosper, not to harm us. God wants his people to thrive!

Simple Summary

1) God honors obedience and faithful stewardship.

2) We should never "give to get." Make sure to give with the right motives.

3) Following Jesus doesn't guarantee prosperity or financial gain.

4) When we are faithful stewards, God blesses us and increases our responsibilities.

5) We can prosper in and through Jesus Christ when we accept his work on the cross.

Chapter 11

TREASURING RELATIONSHIPS

*My command is this:
Love each other as I have loved you.*
—John 15:12

One of the greatest treasures God entrusts to us is the relationships we get to enjoy each day. Relationships can be difficult to maintain at times, but they are worth it. They give life meaning. We all want to win in this area of our lives. Without quality relationships, our enjoyment of life is greatly diminished. Therefore, we are wise to steward them well. In this chapter we will take a look at some of our most important relationships and what God's word tells us about how to relate to others.

Let's start with the family. Satan has been attacking the family for years, knowing that if he can cause chaos in this arena, there will be a ripple effect across other relationships. He attacks men with temptations like pornography, extramarital affairs, and an unhealthy desire to look successful in the world's eyes. He attacks women by making them dislike their appearance, compare themselves to others, and seek worth in something other than Christ. We must be on guard, and we must be intentional if we want our family to thrive.

So what does managing your family in a biblical manner look

like? Strong families spend quality time together. Strong families love each other unconditionally. Strong families pray together. Strong families forgive each other when mistakes are made. Strong families study the Bible together. Strong families enjoy meals together. Strong families encourage openness and honesty in conversation. You get the picture. Satan will have a difficult time breaking down a family that follows these principles.

Parents

The Bible tells us to honor our father and mother. To honor means to have great respect for them. In Ephesians 6:1, Paul tells us, " 'Children, obey your parents in the Lord for this is right.' " Respecting our parents should be the top priority for us in this relationship. It saddens me when I hear of children at odds with their parents. Life is just too short to continue down that road. No set of parents is perfect, but most do the best they can with what they know and what they have. If you aren't on speaking terms with your parents, do everything in your power to mend this relationship. If you have wronged them, ask for forgiveness. If they have wronged you, initiate a conversation around this, and seek forgiveness. Keeping this relationship healthy is imperative to having a thriving family. I recognize that some parental relationships are toxic, and repair may be beyond your control. Romans 12:18 says, "If possible, so far as it depends on you, be at peace with all men." If you find yourself in this situation, pray daily for your parents, and just continue putting your best foot forward.

Spouse

The Bible also has a lot to say about the relationship between a husband and wife. Like the family unit, marriages are under attack. A few years ago, the Supreme Court sent shockwaves through our country by redefining the marriage union. No longer is marriage defined as between one man and one woman. With their historic decision, men can now legally marry men and women can marry women. This is a direct violation of scripture. It is also a violation of God's design for marriage. As time goes on, this blatant disregard to God-ordained marriage will continue to tear away the moral fabric of our country. When little boys are being raised by two women and no father and little girls are brought up by two men and no mother, evil and sin will abound. We must return to the conservative Christian principles on which this country was founded.

Let's further examine what God's word says about the role of a husband and wife. Ephesians 5:22–33 says,

> Wives, submit to your husbands as to the Lord. For the husband is the head of the wife as Christ is the head of the church, his body, of which he is the Savior. Now as the church submits to Christ, so also wives should submit to their husbands in everything. Husbands, love your wives, just as Christ loved the church and gave himself up for her to make her holy, cleansing her by the washing with water through the word, and to present her to himself as a radiant church, without stain or wrinkle or any other blemish, but holy and blameless. In this same way, husbands ought to love their wives as their own bodies. He who loves his wife loves himself. After all, no one ever hated their own body, but they feed and care for their body, just as Christ does the church—for we are members of his body. "For this reason a man will leave his father and mother and be united to his wife, and the two will become one flesh." This is a profound mystery—but I am talking about Christ and the church. However, each one of you also must love his wife as he loves himself, and the wife must respect her husband.

Men, we are called to love our wives as Christ loved the church. Christ gave himself up for the church and laid down his life for her. We too should put aside our own agendas for the good of our spouse. We are called to be providers and protectors. Our role is to love and serve our brides with an unconditional love. We are to be followers of Jesus and lead our families in a Christ-like way. Ladies, scripture tells you to submit to your husband. This isn't a popular teaching today. Submission is frowned upon, as though Paul were saying in this passage that men were better or more valuable than women. That is totally not the case. God created both men and women in his image and his likeness. Both play an incredibly important role in the marriage. Both also play an incredibly important role in God's kingdom. Submission in this sense is identifying leadership in the home. Ultimately, men are held accountable for the direction of the household. A wife is to support her husband as long as he is leading her in a Christ-like way. When the marriage is firing on all cylinders, the man is surrendered to Christ and following him, allowing the wife to properly submit to her husband. It's a beautiful picture of Jesus and his bride, the church.

This scripture also speaks of two becoming one flesh. The male and female bodies were uniquely designed to fit together in sexual union. This consummation of a marriage is a powerful expression of a husband's and wife's love for each other. It is one of God's great gifts to us. However, scripture also declares that this sexual interaction is off-limits to those who aren't married. Our culture has thrown this teaching out the window in favor of whatever feels good. Sexual immorality is at an all-time high and breaks the heart of a holy God. Two becoming one means more than just a physical act. When we are joined together in marriage, we are agreeing to work together in every way. Making decisions together, raising a family together, managing money together, and worshipping together are just a few examples. It is a lifetime commitment to do life together. When done in a biblical manner, it is an incredible blessing from God.

TREASURING RELATIONSHIPS

In summary, men, we are to love our wives. Ladies, you are to respect your husbands. When the marriage is full of love and respect, it thrives. When one is missing, the other will quickly go away. Dr. Emerson Eggerich calls this the crazy cycle. For more on this topic, I recommend his book *Love and Respect*.

Children

Parenting is one of the hardest things most of us will ever face. Someone told me when my boys were born that children bring out every emotion you've ever experienced (and some you haven't yet experienced) all in one little, tiny package. They produce both love and anger. They give us both frustration and patience. They bring us joy and grief. I could go on and on. But parenting is also one of the most rewarding things we can experience in this life. The responsibility of raising children is one of the greatest stewardship opportunities entrusted to us. Children belong to God. They are a gift to us from him. He has control but allows us to mold, shape, and teach them daily. Thankfully, He shares some wisdom on what this looks like in his word:

- Ephesians 6:4: "Fathers, do not exasperate your children; instead, bring them up in the training and instruction of the Lord."
- Proverbs 13:24: "Whoever spares the rod hates their children, but the one who loves their children is careful to discipline them."
- Proverbs 22:6: "Start children off on the way they should go, and even when they are old they will not turn from it."
- 1 Peter 5:2–3: "Be shepherds of God's flock that is under your care, watching over them—not because you must, but because you are willing, as God wants you to be; not pursuing dishonest gain, but eager to

serve; not lording it over those entrusted to you, but being examples to the flock."
- Deuteronomy 6:6–9: "These commandments that I give you today are to be on your hearts. Impress them on your children. Talk about them when you sit at home and when you walk along the road, when you lie down and when you get up. Tie them as symbols on your hands and bind them on your foreheads. Write them on the doorframes of your houses and on your gates."

As parents we are to encourage our children. We are to teach them right and wrong. We are to share God's word with them and help them understand it. When the situation calls for it, it is our responsibility to discipline them. We must spend time with them when they are young and point them in the right direction. And we must be an example to them in the way we live our own lives. Their hearts are tender and fertile. It is our job to plant seeds of truth and love. Our relationship with our children can be an incredibly rich experience if we enact it God's way.

Let's briefly look at some other important relationships and what God tells us about them.

Grandchildren

Proverbs tells us that a wise person leaves an inheritance to his children's children. I believe this speaks to more than just money. Grandparents have the unique responsibility of determining the direction of their family. Decisions made by grandparents have a tremendous impact on the future generations of their family. And what grandfather or grandmother does not want to leave a great legacy for their grandchildren to follow? If you are blessed to be a grandparent, let me encourage you to pass biblical wisdom on to those who look up to you. Spend time with them and teach them life lessons. Share your experiences with them. Share both successes and failures. The best way to leave a powerful legacy is to point your offspring to Christ.

Friends

Hopefully, you have many friends. We all need friends to walk with us through life. The Bible tells us that to have friends we must ourselves be friendly. Be kind to others. Put their interest ahead of your own. And, at times, be prepared to "lay down your life for a friend." You will probably never be asked to give your life for someone else. But all of us will be asked to help someone at some point when we'd rather be doing something else. A true friend loves with a selfless love. If you are blessed with great friendships, you would be wise to steward them well.

Neighbors

Jesus said the second greatest commandment is to love your neighbor as yourself. This was followed by a discussion of "Who is my neighbor?" Each of us have neighbors who are defined as those who live in close proximity to us. We also have neighbors at work, neighbors at church (for those of us who sit on the same pew every Sunday), and neighbors in other areas of our lives. The truth is Jesus calls for us to love everyone. There is an expectation as to how we should treat each other. His word makes that very clear.

Let's assume for a second that Jesus was actually talking about the families who live closest to us. If every Christ-follower just loved and served the four or five families nearest to us, it would change the world. Instead of hiding behind our fences and massive garage doors, what if we invited others into our homes and lives? What if we looked out for each other the way Jesus would look out for us if he were our neighbor? It's a great starting point if you want your family to begin surrendering to this powerful commandment.

Fellow Believers

As the world becomes more and more hostile to Christianity, it is so important for fellow believers to strengthen relationships. We need to continuously encourage each other. Hebrews 10:25 says, "Let us not give up meeting together, as some are in the habit of doing, but let us encourage one another and all the more as you see the day approaching." We need to pray for each other daily. And when one among us has needs, we should be quick to step up and help out. The Christian life can be tough at times, but it is even tougher if lived in isolation. This is exactly how Satan wants it. He is watching the flock and is ready to pounce on any one sheep that strays from the others. Galatians 6 tells us to carry each other's burdens and not to grow weary in doing good, especially for the family of believers.

Nonbelievers

Equally important for followers of Jesus is to not remain in our Christian bubbles, avoiding those who believe differently than us. We are called to be salt and light in the world. We are supposed to be known for our love. Unfortunately, many non-Christians think we are narrow-minded and old-fashioned. We must meet people where they are and show a genuine interest in their well-being. As we develop real relationships with nonbelievers, hopefully they will see that we are different in a good way. Just because someone doesn't share your core beliefs and values doesn't mean they aren't worth loving and pointing to Jesus. Don't run from these opportunities—embrace them. If we are going to reach a lost world, we can't look down our noses at people and condemn them for their sinful behaviors.

Sphere of Influence

One of the powerful truths of relationships is this: there are those in my path whom I have the unique opportunity to impact. Same goes for you—there are people you will encounter that I may never meet. God often brings us to certain places at certain times to make a difference in the life of another person. Will we be ready when that opportunity presents itself? Let's stand ready to love someone in our sphere of influence who needs loving. Let's be prepared to serve a person or family in need. Being the hands and feet of Jesus should be our mission as we journey through this broken world. As the old saying goes, "We may be the only Bible a person will ever read."

There are certain barriers to building deep, meaningful relationships. I am going to touch on three that I think are the most prevalent today:

1) **Busyness**. If we were to be honest, we would all have to admit our lives are just too busy. We run from one thing to another at a record pace and never seem to get caught up. Our children are involved in too many activities, and we find it hard to say no to most anything we are asked to do. If we are not careful, our busyness will keep us occupied while our relationships simultaneously suffer. Make time for those who need you most. Spouses, set aside time for lunch or dinner dates. Parents, turn the television off, put the cell phones down, and enjoy a family meal with your children. Take vacations, and do fun things together. Be very intentional about the things you allow in your calendar each week. If you do not plan your week, the world will plan it for you. Slow down, and enjoy all that God has blessed you with.

2) **Social Media**. I've already touched on this in a previous chapter, so I'll be brief here. If we are not careful, social media will give us a false sense of relationship. "Friends," "likes," and "followers" are not the same as true friendships. A text message isn't the same as

sitting kneecap to kneecap with someone you love discussing important matters. Commenting on their posts doesn't say I love you like meeting them for coffee to hear more about what's going on in their life. I'm amused when I see someone post "HBD" on another's Facebook page to wish them a good birthday. How impersonal can we get? Call me old-fashioned, but I still like to send a card, make a phone call, or even drop by for a visit to let someone know they are special to me. Don't use social media to judge the quality of your friendships. Ask yourself how many people are in your life right now whom you trust completely. How many can you be yourself with even if it means being extremely vulnerable? How many love you unconditionally and have your best interest at heart? The answers to those questions are a much better indicator than Facebook, Instagram, or Twitter.

3) **Our listening skills**. Have you ever been talking to someone and realized they were not paying any attention at all to what you are saying? Sadly, those interactions are becoming more and more normal. Everyone asks you how you are doing, but no one listens (or cares) to hear the answer. People love to talk about themselves. In a normal conversation, many people are thinking more about what they will say next than what the speaker is saying now. Our listening skills just seem to get worse and worse over time. If you really want to build meaningful relationships, work at being a good listener. Show the people in your life you really care about them and what they are saying. Seek to understand before trying to be understood. If you are intentional about this, you will begin to see improvement in the quality of your relationships.

God has given us the beautiful gift of living in relationship with others. He saw that it wasn't good for Adam to be alone, so he created Eve. Relationships will not thrive at all times. We are a broken people. We live in a broken world. Things get messy at times when people are involved. So what is the answer? Surrender. We must surrender our selfishness to a loving God who desires for us to benefit from our relationships with others. Only when we are fully surrendered to the Creator of the human relationship can we genuinely put the interest of others ahead of our own. And when our hearts are aligned with God's plan for our relationships, we will have no choice but to steward them well.

Simple Summary

1) Our relationships are incredible gifts from God.

2) We have a responsibility to steward our relationships well.

3) Satan wants to attack our families and derail our most important relationships.

4) The Bible offers countless nuggets of wisdom on how relationships should work.

5) Busyness, social media, and poor listening skills are potential barriers to healthy relationships.

Section 4:
The Gospel

Chapter 12

THE GREATEST SURRENDER

God's Plan for Our Salvation

> *For God so loved the world that he gave his one and only Son, that whoever believes in him shall not perish but have eternal life.*
>
> —JOHN 3:16

In this final section, we are going to turn our attention to a simple yet powerful truth. What you are about to read could very well be the most important message of this book. Fully surrendering your life to Jesus and being a good steward of his work in your life are foundational for any Christ-follower. Before we take a strong look at God's incredible plan for our salvation, allow me a minute to answer a question you may be asking.

In a book written to Christ-followers on surrender and stewardship, why include a chapter that takes us back to the very basics of Christianity? Here is the answer: because God's wonderful plan for our salvation is at the heart of the Christian faith! There is no way surrender and stewardship can be discussed without including this great Gospel message. It is extremely important for us to be reminded of what we believe, why we believe it, and why it ultimately matters. As believers we need to understand the seriousness of what I am about to cover. We also need to be able to verbalize this plan of salvation in a logical manner when we have opportunities to share it with others.

Our hard-charging personalities and desire to control outcomes makes it difficult to accept God's free gift of salvation. To humbly admit there is nothing I can do to earn salvation and completely trust in Jesus to save us is to go against human nature. I struggled with this for many years. Finally I came to realize this is the way it was designed. Or should I say *the way* it was designed. Jesus said in John 14:6, "I am the way the truth and the life. No one comes to the Father except through me." Ephesians 2:8–9 tells us salvation is "the gift of God, not by works so that no one can boast."

We are saved *for* good works but not *by* our good works. The greatest surrender occurs when we let go of control of our eternal destiny. Salvation is a gift from God. We cannot earn it. We cannot live good enough lives to deserve it. We must trust Jesus for it. As my dad once told me about the moment he gave his life to Christ, "I turned everything over to Jesus and basically told Him, 'If I die and go to hell, I will go there believing in You and what You did for me on the cross. It's in Your hands now.' " That is exactly the place Jesus wants it—in his hands. In this chapter we will further explore salvation and the ultimate victory that comes from this most important surrender.

In the introduction I encouraged those who struggle with doubt to read this chapter. If you are not a fully committed Christ-follower, these next two chapters are really the most important ones for you to ponder. Until you understand God and have a proper view of him and what he has done for you, surrender doesn't make any sense. As long as you feel in control of your own destiny, you probably do not see a need to apply these principles. And if you live life with your fists tightly wrapped around "your stuff," stewardship is likely a foreign concept.

The first act of surrender occurs when a new believer gives

their life to Christ. It is a decision to turn from their current way of living and embrace a new direction. The old is gone, and the new is being ushered in. Some call it being saved. Others may use the terms redeemed, set free, following Christ, or washed in the blood. All these are true. It is the greatest moment in the life of any Christian. It is the most important thing that anyone can ever decide to do. Salvation occurs when a sinner recognizes their need of a savior, repents of their sin, and makes Jesus Christ the Lord of their life. At that moment, we let go of control and lean on God's plan for our life. We place our faith and trust in the only One who is truly faithful and trustworthy. He will not fail us, nor ever let us down. That is the Gospel. Through him and him alone can we win in the end.

Gospel literally means "good news." In a broken world where selfishness, greed, and division are the norm, we could all use some good news. What you are about to read is the best news you will ever hear. It all started thousands of years ago, shortly after God spoke the universe into existence. I have already touched on Genesis 1:1, in which God created the heavens and the earth. God was present at the beginning of time. As a matter of fact, he created time. The first few chapters of the Bible go into detail about the creation of all things. Therefore, we can rest in the knowledge that there is a Creator that made us, loves us, and has the world in the palm of his hand. Genesis literally means the origin or beginning of something. What was originating in this first book of the Bible was the greatest plan ever drawn up.

Genesis 1:27: "So God created man in His own image, in the image of God He created him; male and female He created them." God made man in his own image. We are his pride and joy. God made us to worship him, have fellowship with him, and walk in perfect peace and harmony with him. As a side note, the second part of this verse states God created us as male and female. We live in a world today that seems to be having a gender identity crisis. Maybe this biblical truth will help. We can't decide we are something different than God created us to be. A male is a male, and a female is a female. Our birth gender is the only gender we will ever be, and no surgery or procedure can ever change that. To attempt to go against God's design for humanity is sin. "What is sin?" you ask. Disobeying God is sin, and this is exactly what Adam and Eve did shortly after creation. Sin is rebellion and is the opposite of surrender. We move on to Genesis 3.

In Genesis 3 man sinned against God. Adam and Eve did the one thing that God had specifically asked them not to do. They failed to obey God's initial instructions, something we all do regularly. Because of this initial sin, we are all born sinners and separated from God. Mankind's perfect fellowship with God was broken on the day that Adam and Eve disobeyed God.

Romans 3:23: "For all have sinned and fall short of the glory of God." No one is without sin (except Jesus). No matter how hard we try, we cannot earn God's favor. We now live in a broken world. Each of us falls short every day. Our natural inclinations are to please ourselves and not God. Each person's sinful tendencies may be different. One person may struggle with pride and greed while the next person may struggle with sexual temptation. The enemy (more on him later) knows our weaknesses and vulnerabilities. He attacks us in the areas where he has the best chance of causing us to fail.

Romans 5:12: "Therefore just as sin entered the world through one man, and death through sin, and in this way, death came to all men because all sinned." Sin entered the world through the disobedience of Adam and Eve. The death being referred to here is more than a natural death. We are dead in our sins. We are spiritually cut off from God. If we continue down this road, we will be eternally separated from God in a place called hell. That's the bad news. Ready for the good news?

Romans 6:23: "For the wages of sin is death, but the gift of

God is eternal life through Christ Jesus our Lord." There is victory in Jesus! What we deserved for our sins was death. But God made a way! God gave us a gift in the form of his son. Through Jesus Christ we can have eternal life (heaven) and a beginning here on this earth. This is the Gospel!

John 3:16: "For God so loved the world that he gave His one and only Son that whoever believes in Him shall not perish but have eternal life." Jesus came into this world, lived a perfect life, and died for our sins. He paid the price for *our* sins. He also came back to life three days later and went back to heaven to be with his father. This is a critical truth. If Jesus had not risen from the dead, faith in him would be completely in vain. 1 Corinthians 15:14 tells us, "If Christ has not been raised, our preaching is useless and so is our faith." Thankfully, the grave could not hold him. He defeated death by walking out of his tomb alive. Through Jesus and because of his great sacrifice, we can once again have fellowship with God and a relationship with our Creator. Jesus paid it all! All we need to do is accept his work on the cross on our behalf.

Romans 10:9: "That if you confess with your mouth that Jesus is Lord and believe in your heart that God raised Him from the dead, you will be saved." Salvation occurs when we admit that we are sinners, believe in Jesus, and accept his sacrifice on the cross as payment for our sins. We are surrendering our lives to God and committing to following him for life. When we are saved, the Holy Spirit comes into our heart and lives within us. The spirit will guide our lives if we allow him to. We are now set apart to be used for his kingdom causes and participate in his kingdom work.

Salvation isn't the end of the journey. It's only the beginning! After giving our lives to Jesus, we begin walking on a path toward spiritual maturity. This is called sanctification. Our goal now is to become Christlike in every way. Our thoughts, words, and actions should now be filtered through a biblical filter. Surrendering to Christ as our Lord and Savior does not mean that life gets easy and we are now on cruise control. Our fleshly desires still rear their ugly heads daily. God's word speaks directly to this power struggle.

Galatians 5:16–25 tells us:

> So I say, walk by the Spirit, and you will not gratify the desires of the flesh. For the flesh desires what is contrary to the Spirit, and the Spirit what is contrary to the flesh. They are in conflict with each other, so that you are not to do whatever you want. But if you are led by the Spirit, you are not under the law.
>
> The acts of the flesh are obvious: sexual immorality, impurity and debauchery; idolatry and witchcraft; hatred, discord, jealousy, fits of rage, selfish ambition, dissensions, factions and envy; drunkenness, orgies, and the like. I warn you, as I did before, that those who live like this will not inherit the kingdom of God.
>
> But the fruit of the Spirit is love, joy, peace, patience, kindness, goodness, faithfulness, gentleness and self-control. Against such things there is no law. Those who belong to Christ Jesus have crucified the flesh with its passions and desires. Since we live by the Spirit, let us keep in step with the Spirit.

We can follow our fleshly desires or be led by the Spirit of God. Our lifestyles are a direct reflection of which one we have chosen. We must allow God's Spirit to guide us. Surrendering to his still, small voice allows our lives to be an example to those whom God places in front of us each day. We also must study his word and obey it. The Bible is rich with wisdom straight from our Heavenly Father. We are his creation, and his word is our owner's manual. Others should begin to see Jesus in us by the way we live our lives.

Matthew 7:17–20: "Every good tree bears good fruit, but a bad tree bears bad fruit. Thus, by their fruit, you will recognize them." If we are firmly planted in the word of God and are allowing his love to flow through us, our lives will produce good fruit. Good fruit is pleasant, healthy, and desirable. Bad fruit is distasteful, undesirable, and ultimately worthless. A life lived for Jesus produces good fruit. You may be asking, "Why does all this even matter? Can't I just try to live a decent life and not have to worry about any of this stuff?" Let me allow scripture to answer those questions.

Matthew 7:13–14: "Enter through the narrow gate. For wide is the gate and broad is the road that leads to destruction, and many enter through it. But small is the gate and narrow the road that leads to life, and only a few find it." There are only two paths. Unfortunately, many folks will take the wide road. The wide road is the way of the world. It is following your fleshly desires. It is the road that leads directly to hell. However, those who follow Jesus on the narrow path will find life, both in this world and the next. Eternal life for the Christian is spent in heaven. Heaven is a place that will be simply amazing and beyond our wildest dreams.

1 Corinthians 2:9: "No eye has seen, no ear has heard, and no human mind has conceived the things God has prepared for those who love him." Heaven is a place of perfect love, perfect peace, and perfect joy. It is a place where the believers will live forever and ever worshipping the King of Kings and the Lord of Lords. In heaven there will be no pain, sickness, sorrow, or death. And yes, heaven is biblical.

In John 14:2-3 Jesus said, " 'My Father's house has many rooms; if that were not so, I would have told you. I am going there to prepare a place for you and if I go and prepare a place for you I will come back and take you to be with me that you also may be where I am.' " I once heard an old preacher say, "Jesus was a carpenter while on Earth, and He has been gone a long time. There is no telling what size mansion He has built for us!" In all seriousness, heaven is real, and it is above human comprehension.

Revelation tells us he will wipe every tear from our eyes. No longer will there be any mourning, any curse, or any night. It will be all good all the time!

Pastor Randy Alcorn has this to say about heaven: "In order to better understand the beauty of Heaven, just look all around you. And then remove all sin, death, suffering, and corruption." He goes on to say that no conversation about heaven is complete without a discussion around God's presence in heaven and our relationship with him. "Being with God and seeing His face is the central joy of Heaven and the source of all other joys."[1]

So if the small gate and the narrow road lead to heaven, then what exactly is hell and this other road? This is a question that demands a straight answer. What I am about to say is not intended to scare you. It is biblical truth that every person needs to hear. Hell is a real place. It is not some fictional place that makes for great cartoons and entertainment. Hell is a place of eternal punishment. It is awaiting those who reject Jesus and never turn from their sins.

Revelation 20:15: "Anyone whose name was not found written in the book of life was thrown into the lake of fire." Allow me to paraphrase the verse you just read: if you aren't a Christ-follower, you will be thrown into a place of eternal suffering.

Matthew 25:41: "Then he will say to those on the left, depart from me you who are cursed into the eternal fire prepared for the devil and his angels." It is worth saying one more time. Those who do not know Jesus as their Lord and Savior will spend eternity in a lake of fire, forever separated from God. Think for just a second about a time when you have touched an oven that was heated to 350 degrees. The instant painful sensation causes you to throw your hand back and scream. It may even leave a blister on your hand. Now imagine if someone placed you inside of this oven

---

[1] Randy Alcorn, *Heaven* (Carol Stream, Illinois: Tyndale House Publishers, 2004).

and left you there. The pain would be unbearable, and you would be dead in a short amount of time. Now consider this: What if the pain never went away and you remained alive in that torture chamber? Forever. And ever. And ever. Never-ending. Constant excruciating pain. With no end in sight. Eternal separation. And punishment. Forever. Such will be the reality for those who die without Jesus.

Again, I am not trying to scare anyone. This is what the Bible teaches. If you profess to be a Christian, this is a good time to make sure you have it right. We are to "work out our salvation with fear and trembling." Allow this to also serve as an important reminder of what's at stake for those around us who are lost.

Matthew 7:21–23 warns us that not all who think their eternity is secure will be correct. On judgment day he will say to them, "Away from me, you evildoers. I never knew you." Don't fool yourself. What are you relying on for salvation? If it is anything other than Jesus, you may be on the wrong path. And if you have never fully surrendered your life to Christ, now is the time. Today is the day of salvation. Don't put if off. Give your life to Christ, and you will be eternally grateful.

There are many religions and scholars today that teach multiple ways to be saved and multiple paths to heaven. They say we are narrow-minded. Yes, we are! The Bible tells us the road leading to life is narrow. Jesus narrows it down even more in John 14:6:

"I am *the* way, and *the* truth, and *the* life. No one comes to the Father except through *Me*." Jesus dispels this "multiple ways" myth with one profound truth. He is *the* way. Not *a* way. *The* way. In the second part of this verse, he uses the words "no one." This doesn't leave any wiggle room for a person to slide around his declaration. He ends the statement with the word "Me." This is obviously referring to Jesus because he is the one doing the talking. If you believe the Bible, this verse should give you full confidence that Jesus truly is the only way to salvation.

As wonderful as this plan of salvation is, I am ashamed to admit that I rejected it for many years. I was twenty-two years old when I finally surrendered to Jesus and made him Lord of my life. I grew up in a Christian home and heard good preaching on a weekly basis. From age five to age twenty-two, I could quote John 3:16 and tell anyone who asked exactly what it took to be saved. However, I never fully accepted this great gift that Jesus was offering me. Many times I prayed a prayer then opened my eyes to see if I felt any different. Time and time again, I was disappointed and wondered why God hadn't saved me.

During a revival service on a warm summer evening in 2001, I saw God in a way I had never seen him before. I finally realized that it wasn't about how hard I tried or how well I could pray. The work had already been done on the cross! My role in salvation was actually quite simple. *Quit trying to help God save me. Surrender my life to him. Believe and receive.* I had always believed. But that night I surrendered and received his free gift of salvation. I became a new creation that night. My heart now had true peace, and my eternal destination was sealed. My life has never been the same since letting Jesus take control.

A common question regarding salvation is "How young is too young for someone to give their life to Christ?" I certainly do not have all the answers as it relates to this topic, but I can joyfully share a personal story with you. I mentioned in a previous chapter that I am the proud father of twin boys, Max and Miles. When Miles was seven years old, he began asking questions about God, heaven, and hell. He told us often that he wanted to give his life to Jesus and make sure he would go to heaven if he died. We sought counsel from our pastor on how to best handle his questions. Our pastor told us to answer his questions as openly and honestly as we could but not pressure him or force him to make a decision.

This continued for months, with Miles asking questions and saying he wanted to be saved. We walked him through the plan of salvation (as outlined in this chapter) and answered each question to the best of our abilities. One night as we were again discussing how to receive God's free gift of salvation, Miles stopped us and said, "But, Daddy and Mommy, I've already done that! I'm ready to be baptized!"

A few weeks later, Miles told us he planned to make a public profession of faith and join the church on Sunday. We asked him to pray that night and see if he still had peace in his heart when he woke up the next morning. When my wife woke him up for church that Sunday, Miles said, "Mommy, I promised God last night I would walk the aisle today, and I am not breaking that promise!"

Later that morning, with a huge grin on his face, Miles Broome walked down the aisle and told the church about his commitment to give his life to Jesus. He was eight years old at the time, and I fully believe he is now a born-again child of God. He loves Jesus, loves people, and has a great heart. Does he fully understand all there is to know about the Christian life? No. But guess what? I don't either, and neither do you. As our children's minister explained to us, Miles is saying yes to what he understands today about Jesus. If Jesus is tugging at your heartstrings and drawing you to him, I encourage you, too, to say yes. It doesn't matter if you are eight or eighty.

As you engage in conversations about the Christian faith, you will hear many different reasons people do not embrace Christianity. Here are some of the most common, with my personal thoughts about each one:

1) "The Christians I know are hypocrites." Unfortunately, this statement has more truth in it than we care to admit. Many professed Christ-followers behave the same way nonbelievers behave. Also, we have made a big deal of the things we are against instead of promoting the things we are all about. We have judged

those who do or believe certain things instead of loving them with a Christlike love. However, here is a truth you need to know about all Christians. We are no better than you! We are sinners who screw up every day. God was gracious enough to forgive us, and we were humble enough to accept his forgiveness. We are anything but perfect, so don't judge a perfect God by the actions of imperfect people.

2) "Churches just want my money. And I really don't fit in there anyway." The church should be a place where we can go to worship, serve, and find community. Yes, the church needs money to keep the doors open. But that is not what a body of believers is all about. When we speak of giving money to the church, it is an act of obedience that releases the grip money has on our lives. God doesn't need our money. He wants our hearts. The church is full of sinners, no matter how they dress, act, or look. Anyone should be welcome anytime!

3) "Christians are weird." I sure hope so! We are called to be different. Following the teachings of Christ goes against the grain of our culture today. We are called to be light in a dark world. A Christ-follower should stand out in a good way.

4) "I don't want to stop drinking, cursing, or being sexually active." As previously mentioned, we are all sinners. We all struggle with different fleshly desires. Giving your life to Christ doesn't make all temptations go away. It does, however, give you a new source of power to fight against bad habits. Following biblical principles is freeing as it gives you better guidelines for how to live. Also, following Jesus will change your heart, which will lead to positive changes in behavior.

5) "I'm too smart to believe all those crazy Bible stories. That stuff didn't really happen." This is becoming a more and more common reason people walk away from the faith. If this describes you, let me encourage you to focus on the life of Jesus and his resurrection. This is the foundation of the Christian faith. Do your own research, and arrive at your own conclusions about Christianity. I think you will be pleasantly surprised at what you uncover as you study Jesus.

As I went through God's plan for our salvation, I used a lot of scripture and lot of Jesus's teachings. But many people do not believe the Bible and fully subscribe to its teachings. How do we overcome this barrier and get people to understand and embrace God's holy word? Hopefully, this next chapter will help you see and explain God's beautiful storybook in a different way.

Simple Summary

1) Our sin separates us from God.

2) Jesus gave his life on our behalf. He paid the price for our sins.

3) Heaven is a real place prepared for those who follow Jesus.

4) Hell awaits those who reject Jesus as Lord.

5) Salvation is available to all who repent, turn from their sins, and surrender to Jesus as their personal Savior.

Chapter 13

IS THE BIBLE TRUE?

*All Scripture is God-breathed
and is useful for teaching, rebuking, correcting
and training in righteousness.*
—2 Timothy 3:16

Earlier this year I had an unexpected debate with an atheist. It was on a Saturday afternoon, and my wife and I were wrapping up a weekend visit to a friend's house in Chicago. As we were sitting around the living room chatting, the group conversation went from politics to religion. As I listened to each person in the room share their views, I couldn't help but notice that one person had a very different worldview than all the others. Seth (not his real name) resisted anything related to the Bible and was obviously less conservative in his thinking.

As I sat there prayerfully considering how to share my faith with him, he laid a golden opportunity at my feet. "I just do not believe that what you guys are saying is true," Seth proclaimed. "We will just have to agree to disagree."

In that moment I felt the Holy Spirit telling me to speak up. "So, Seth, if you don't mind me asking, what exactly do you believe?" Seth's answer began an intense but friendly two-hour conversation about his beliefs, my beliefs, God's word, and Christianity.

"I believe in me" was his reply. "I believe in my own ability to make things happen and control the space around me. I believe when I die, I become maggot food, and the legacy I leave is based on the way I treated people while I was alive."

Yikes! My heart immediately became heavy at the hopelessness of this belief system. So I shared with him the hope I have in Jesus and the eternal life that is promised.

His response: "I wish I believed that. I really do. I can see where that would make life a lot easier, especially when times are tough. But I'm too smart to embrace that way of thinking. Science disproves the Bible."

"So what do you believe about Jesus?" I asked.

He said, "I think he was a good man who brainwashed a lot of people. I think the reason Christianity still exists is because Jesus was an incredible salesman who convinced a bunch of people to believe a bunch of lies."

Our conversation took many twists and turns but ultimately ended with me sharing this thought: "Seth, if you are not one hundred and ten percent convinced that you are correct, I implore you to go back and consider whether Jesus really was the son of God. And here's why: If you are right and I am wrong, then when we die, we are both okay. And I've actually tried to live a good moral life based on the teachings of Jesus, which you agreed were very solid. I've tried to love others, serve others, and be generous with my time and money. However—and this is a huge however—what if I'm right and you're wrong? That means I get to spend eternity in a place of paradise called heaven. That means this life was just preparation for the next. For thousands and millions and billions of years, I will enjoy living in a perfect place with the Creator of the universe. And you? I have some horrible news for you. If I'm right and you are wrong, you will enter hell the minute you die. Hell is a place of suffering that is *never* quenched. It is prepared for the devil and his angels. It is prepared for those who reject Jesus. And I would not be telling you this if I didn't love you and

IS THE BIBLE TRUE?

want you to join me in heaven. So, Seth, if there is even .00001% doubt in your mind about what you believe to be true, please go back and study the life, death, and resurrection of Jesus."

We parted ways on a friendly note. I shared my testimony with him, then he hugged me and told me I seemed like a good man. I challenged him to consider the evidence for the resurrection, read the testimony of the eyewitnesses, and call me if I could help in any way. As I traveled back home that evening, my heart was overflowing. The conversation had been challenging but invigorating. I thanked God for giving me the words to say and the tone in which he had allowed me to say them. But deep down I realized that I needed to be more prepared to "give a reason for the hope that I have."

There are many people today who, like Seth, do not believe the Bible to be true. It is one of the most misunderstood documents of all time, especially among those who do not profess faith in Christ. This chapter will outline some basic principles that should help you in your "Seth conversations." And hopefully these truths will strengthen your faith as well and help you be better prepared to defend your beliefs. For a much deeper look at the Bible and how it came to be, I highly recommend Pastor Andy Stanley's sermon series titled, "The Bible for Grown-Ups." I also recommend Lee Strobel's best-selling book, *The Case for Christ*. These resources were very instrumental in shaping my thinking around this topic. Let's start with the following questions:

What exactly is the Bible, and how did it come into existence? The International Bible Society defines the Bible as the account of God's action in the world and his purpose with all creation.[1] More specifically, it is a collection of sixty-six books written over sixteen centuries by over forty different authors and compiled in the late fourth century. Based on this date of compilation, here

---

1 International Bible Society, (*Biblica.com. What is the Bible?*).

is an important fact to consider: The document we now call the Bible did not create Christianity—Christianity actually created the Bible. Yes, the Bible is the inspired word of God. In it, God progressively reveals himself and his purposes. But unlike the starting point for most world religions, the Bible wasn't a book written by some random author *to create* a new religion. The Bible was written by many people over thousands of years and ultimately compiled *because of* what God was doing in the world. It was also the exact message that God wanted to communicate to the world.

Why is this important? The entire Bible did not exist when Jesus walked the earth. Only what we now call our Old Testament was available at that time. The Old Testament writings laid the groundwork for the coming of Jesus. The Old Testament pointed to the cross and to the event that changed everything. That event was the death, burial, and resurrection of Jesus Christ, which served as the foundation of the Christian faith. Because of what many people had witnessed, a movement was started that still exists today.

What did they witness? Here are the details. During his time on earth, Jesus claimed to be God. He even predicted his own death and resurrection. Many people embraced Jesus as the Messiah and chose to follow Him. However, he was a polarizing figure. Others despised him and wanted to get rid of him. His claims of being the personification of the God of the Old Testament did not sit well with a lot of important people. Therefore, something terrible happened. He was arrested, beaten, and killed. For his followers, all hope was gone. Their King was dead.

Because Jesus had predicted his death and resurrection, those who killed him placed soldiers outside his tomb to guard the body. The disciples who followed Jesus were scared. They hunkered down, fearing they would be the next ones put to death. Then something miraculous happened. The same Jesus they had seen being crucified reappeared to them. He had been raised from the dead! He was alive! And more importantly, he was who he had said he was. He appeared to more than five hundred people before he ascended back to heaven. What the early Christians witnessed was a resurrected Savior. This started a movement that could not be stopped. Christ was alive! And so was Christianity. Back to the Bible.

Many eyewitnesses wrote about what they saw. Matthew, Mark, Luke, John, Peter, and James are not just "books of the Bible." These were six men who spent time with Jesus both before and after he died. Nothing was going to stop the faith they now had in their resurrected King. So they carefully documented the life of Jesus and what they witnessed. Their writings are historical treasures. And their writings would eventually be compiled in what we now call our New Testament, along with the writings of another converted eyewitness named Paul.

Paul was a Jew. He was a Pharisee. And he was bound and determined to stop the spread of Christianity in the first century. He persecuted Christ's followers and even helped in putting some to death. But when the risen Christ appeared to him after the resurrection, everything changed. The number-one opponent of the spreading of the Gospel of Jesus became the number-one missionary of all time. Paul traveled from city to city preaching the Gospel and helping people understand what had taken place. He wrote numerous letters to different churches, encouraging and challenging people in their faith. You may have heard of these letters. They are called Romans, Corinthians, Galatians, Ephesians, Philippians, Colossians, Thessalonians, Timothy, Titus, and Philemon. His letters were preserved and became a vital source of information for future Christians. They were eventually joined with the writings of the other eyewitnesses to form the New Testament.

So we have many eyewitnesses who documented exactly what they saw and experienced with Jesus. It is also important to note that these writings were completed not long after Jesus died. Even the weakest evidence points to the fact that the four Gospels (Matthew, Mark, Luke, and John) were written no later than fifty to sixty years after his death. The more likely scenario is a timeline of around thirty after his death. This is important for a couple of reasons: 1) Not enough time had passed for a legend to form. This event was still fresh on the minds of many people. 2) There were plenty of people still living who could have easily disputed their writings if they had not been true. It is believed (based on solid evidence) that most of Paul's writings were written before the writings of Matthew, Mark, Luke, and John. Paul's writing ministry likely started within ten to fifteen years of Jesus dying. And most historians agree that Paul's first letter to the church at Corinth contained information that he received at a meeting with eyewitnesses two to three years after the resurrection! To put this in perspective, Alexander the Great's biographies were written four hundred years after he died. And, interestingly enough, these writings about his life are generally considered true and reliable.

So what happens next? These letters and eyewitness accounts described the life of Christ and reveal the birth and development of the early church. The documents were preserved and protected and eventually became sacred scripture. Even during the times when Christianity was under attack, the early believers clung to what they knew about Jesus from these documents. "Under attack" may not be a strong enough phrase. Christians were heavily persecuted. There were early decrees in place to destroy Christians and keep them from meeting together during most of the first three centuries. And these decrees called for all Christian literature to be destroyed. But even in the face of such adversity, the good news of Jesus Christ continued to spread. This should not come as a surprise. The prophet Isaiah had proclaimed hundreds of years earlier that the grass may wither and the flowers may fade, but the word of God would stand forever.

IS THE BIBLE TRUE?

Christianity was multiplying daily. There were thousands of believers in Jesus. Then something happened that changed everything. In the fourth century, the Roman emperor, Constantine, canceled the decrees and allowed Christians to worship freely.[2] For the very first time, Christian scholars could come together and work on organizing the sacred writings. And, in an ironic twist, the Roman Empire, which had been responsible for the death of Jesus, helped fund the collecting and copying of these writings. Thus the first completed version of the Bible was formed! Isn't that amazing?

That gives you an idea of how we got our New Testament. But as you probably know, these New Testament writings were combined with other documents to create our modern-day version of the Holy Bible. "What other documents?" you ask. Today we call those documents the Old Testament. The Old Testament consists of thirty-nine books, mostly about the laws, history, and prophecy of the ancient people of Israel. This Jewish text was known in ancient times as the Law and the Prophets. It also included wisdom literature. The Old Testament is a story of redemption. It documents a covenant God had with his chosen people, the nation of Israel. In many ways the Old Testament lays a foundation for the New Testament. It begins to unveil God's rescue plan for humanity. It points directly to the coming of Jesus.

In the book of Genesis, written by a man named Moses, the creation story is told. It is important to note that Moses wasn't necessarily trying to tell us exactly *how* God created the world. He was mainly trying to let us know *that* God created the world. Also, in the book of Genesis, we learn how sin entered the world through Adam and Eve. God opens our eyes in Genesis to how he feels about sin. Man became so sinful that God flooded the earth,

---

2 Andy Stanley, *The Bible for Grown-Ups* (North Point Community Church, October 2018).

wiping out most of mankind. Moses also wrote Exodus, Leviticus, Numbers, and Deuteronomy. Most of these Old Testament books document the journey of the Israelites struggling through life, clinging to their God—Yahweh.[3]

The Old Testament contains books of history, books of poetry, and books of prophecy. Whereas the New Testament was written after Jesus died and looks back on his life, the Old Testament looks ahead and points to a coming messiah. It is truly fascinating how all these ancient documents, written by many different authors, fit together and unite in a common message.

The writings of the Old Testament are important. There are several things you need to know about these writings. As previously mentioned, they were the only scriptures that existed during Jesus's life. Many times in the New Testament, he refers back to Old Testament scripture. When Jesus was tempted by the devil, he combated Satan's advances by quoting scripture from the Old Testament. One of the reasons we believe so strongly in the Old Testament is because Jesus believed it to be true.

Second, it shows time and time again that God provides for and takes care of his people. Many stories in the Old Testament are very encouraging and motivating to read. Whether it was God parting the Red Sea, David defeating Goliath, or Daniel peacefully sleeping in a den of hungry lions, we see evidence of God protecting his people time and time again. Lastly, the Old Testament pointed directly to Jesus. Many of the laws and Old Testament rituals foreshadowed what Jesus would ultimately do. Sacrifices were a huge part of old covenant living. Jesus became the ultimate sacrifice when he died on the cross. He fulfilled the law and the prophecies and issued in a new covenant based on love and grace. The new covenant applies to all people, not just a select group.

---

3 Stanley, *The Bible for Grown-Ups*.

IS THE BIBLE TRUE?

Therefore, the Bible is made up of the old writings of the Hebrew people combined with the new writings of the early Christians. It is important to note that not all writings during this time made it into the Holy Bible. There were strict criteria for what was to be included in the final version. One important qualification for inclusion was that the writing had to be inspired by God. When we pick up our neatly bound, perfectly printed, leather-covered Bible, we should be very thankful. And we should be very encouraged because Christianity flourished for hundreds of years without what we have today.

In 2010, I went to Ethiopia on a mission trip. I had an eye-opening interaction with one of the local recent converts. He asked me if I owned a Bible. When I shared with him how many Bibles I owned, he smiled from ear to ear. "That is incredible! You are so lucky," he said. "So, you can just walk into a store and buy a new copy of the Bible?" I left that encounter with heavy feelings of guilt. I have in my possession pieces of historical gold. Actually, they are worth far more than gold. The early Christians risked their lives protecting and preserving these treasured documents. Many gave their lives for the cause. And sadly some of us let our Bibles sit on end tables propping up lamps and collecting dust.

No, the Bible wasn't written by Jesus. But it was written about Jesus by many people who walked with Jesus. No, the Bible wasn't written by perfect people. But it was written by people inspired by God. No, the Bible itself is not the foundation of our faith. But it carefully documents the life of the person (Jesus) and the event (his death and resurrection) that is the foundation of our faith. As a matter of fact, most of what we know about Jesus is found in this holy book. Today, everything we believe as Christians is based on the Bible. The primary way God communicates with us is through his word. The Bible is the inerrant word of God. It is a vital part of the life of any Christ-follower. The Bible is true!

So what do you do with this information? If you are a follower of Jesus, hopefully this gives you confidence in the Bible and how it came to be. I pray that it also helps you better understand the foundation and focal point of our faith. If you still have doubts about the existence of God and still aren't fully convinced the Bible is true (or relevant), this next section is for you.

Do you know everything there is to know about the entire universe? Obviously the answer is no. So if no one knows all there is to know about the entire universe, that leaves the door open for the possibility of a God that exists. With that in mind, the only way to proceed is with the facts. Let's look at some of the key facts.

As previously mentioned, the life of Jesus, his death on a cross, and his resurrection are the cornerstone of the Christian faith. So what are the facts surrounding this roughly thirty-three-year period when Jesus walked the earth?

1) No one disputes the fact that Jesus was a real historical figure and amassed quite a following during his time on earth. Even if you look outside of the Bible, you will find evidence of Jesus's life and death. Tacitus, one of the most important Roman historians of the first century, wrote about Jesus. Josephus, a Jewish priest, scholar, and historian also wrote about the life of Jesus. Jesus isn't some fictitious character. There is overwhelming evidence that he did exist. Jesus is real.
2) Jesus died by crucifixion at the hands of the Roman authorities. Again, this fact isn't even disputed by non-Christian scholars and historians.
3) Jesus's tomb was empty. His own opponents even acknowledged the body was missing. They accused the disciples of stealing it. The question wasn't "Is the tomb empty?" The question was "What happened to the body?" This fact is agreed upon by most

historians, both Christian and non-Christian. Also, if the tomb still contained a body, it could have easily been proven by many people who could have gone there to check it out for themselves. When you study the evidence, the most logical conclusion is that Jesus emerged victorious over death and the grave.

4) There were over five hundred eyewitnesses to a resurrected Jesus. He appeared to many people who had spent time with him before he died. This is huge! The same disciples who watched him die saw him, touched him, and hung out with him after He came back to life.

5) The lives of all who saw him again changed forever. Peter went from denying he knew Jesus out of fear for his life to proclaiming the Gospel in the face of heavy persecution. James, the half-brother of Jesus, went from serious doubt to being a respected church leader. Paul, who had an encounter with Jesus after his ascension, went from killing Christians to stop the spread of Christianity to being Christianity's greatest advocate. The disciples went from complete hopelessness after Jesus died to being fully committed Christ-followers. They literally gave their lives for what they had witnessed. There isn't a logical explanation for their behavior other than that they saw something that completely changed their minds and hearts.

6) From the convictions of these new believers, the early church was started. They witnessed something that set in motion a movement that continues to this very day. Billions of people now profess Jesus as Lord of their lives. Christianity is alive and well. The church is still thriving, and the Gospel continues to make its way to the ends of the earth.

Surrendering to WIN

Some try to discredit the eyewitness accounts and the ancient manuscripts. Many arguments have been voiced to try and punch holes in these early writings in an attempt to disprove Christianity. Here is something to consider: There are a total of over sixty-four thousand biblical manuscripts (handwritten copies of the original) in existence. The New Testament accounts for over twenty-seven thousand of those manuscripts. Without anything to compare these numbers to, we aren't sure if this is a lot or not. Let me add more details to shed some light on this information. No other historical document has anywhere close to the same number of manuscripts backing it. Number two on the list would be Homer's *Iliad*. And how many manuscripts are there for this document? Only eighteen hundred! To quote best-selling author and Christian speaker Lee Strobel, "There is an avalanche of historical information supporting the claims of Jesus Christ."[4] Strobel, who was once an atheist, concluded that it would require much more faith to remain a nonbeliever than to surrender to the Gospel of Jesus Christ.

One final thing: How do those old Jewish writings fit together with the new writings that document the life of Jesus? In those old scriptures, there were more than three hundred major predictions (prophecies). Do you know how many of them eventually came to be? Keep in mind many of them were written more than one thousand years before Jesus arrived on planet Earth. I'm sure you can guess the answer. One hundred percent of these predictions came to fruition. The old Jewish "Law and the Prophets" pointed to a coming messiah—a savior of the world. Jesus fulfilled the old covenant. He was born of a virgin and lived a perfect life. He died by crucifixion. Jesus issued a new covenant. Salvation was made available to anyone who believed in Jesus and received his

---

4 Lee Strobel, *The Case for Christ* (Grand Rapids, Michigan: Zondervan, 1998).

IS THE BIBLE TRUE?

free gift of eternal life. The ultimate victory was made possible because of his death on the cross. So considering everything we have discussed in this chapter, is the Bible true? Yes! It is a book inspired by the one true God. Its words are powerful and relevant to us today. The book of Hebrews tells us it is "alive and active and sharper than a double-edged sword." If you are still not convinced, I encourage you to go do your own research. I think you will be pleasantly surprised at what you find.

And if you are wondering about my new friend, Seth, I have sent him several resources to help him discover truth for himself. He is seeking, and I believe God is working in his heart. It would not surprise me if Seth became a Christ-follower. Here was my final charge to him: Focus on Jesus. Focus on His life and death. Then focus on the resurrection. Peter and Paul did not experience life-change because of dinosaur bones, archaeological evidence, or even because Noah built a boat. Their lives changed forever when they encountered a resurrected Jesus. My prayer for Seth is that soon he, too, will encounter the resurrected Jesus.

As we conclude this chapter, here is the ultimate question: What does the Holy Bible ask us to do? If we are truly Christ-followers, we only have one option. Obey it and surrender everything to the One who gave his life for us. His word serves as a light for the path ahead. We must walk in faith, trusting him every step of the way. He is a good God.

There are, however, some very specific things his word tells us about being a follower of Jesus. Quite possibly the most important one is the command Jesus left with his disciples the final time they were together. It is often called the great commission and can be found in Matthew 28:16–20. In the next chapter, we will unpack this charge to followers of Jesus.

Surrendering to WIN

Simple Summary

1) The New Testament was written by people who knew Jesus personally. These men walked with him, talked with him, and were witnesses to his life.

2) The Old Testament includes the Mosaic law, the writings of the prophets, and wisdom literature. The Old Testament foretold the coming of Jesus.

3) The momentum of the early church was based on the life, death, and resurrection of Jesus. This still serves as the foundation of the Christian faith.

4) The writings that make up our modern-day Bible have survived for thousands of years despite heavy persecution in the first few centuries.

5) There is a considerable amount of data supporting the veracity of scripture.

Chapter 14

THE GREATEST STEWARDSHIP
God's Plan for His Gospel

> *Therefore, go and make disciples of all nations, baptizing them in the name of the Father and of the Son and of the Holy Spirit, and teaching them to obey everything I have commanded you. And surely, I am with you always, to the very end of the age.*
>
> —MATTHEW 28:19–20

We have discussed what is required to be saved. God's incredible plan to send his son into the world made salvation possible for all who believe. God's holy word was given to us as a timeless gift to study and through which to gain a greater understanding of God and his character. There is sweet victory found in surrendering our lives to the lordship of Jesus. Now what? What do I do if I have trusted in Jesus, own a copy of the Bible, and want to live a life that pleases him? The answer to this question deserves a book of its own. In fact, many great ones have been written. Let me begin by sharing what your next steps should *not* look like.

I'm afraid many people view their salvation as fire insurance. I do not want to "burn in hell forever," so I am going to trust Jesus to keep me out of that awful place. I have no plans of changing anything about the way I live. I just need Jesus to come along for the ride and be there for me when I need him. Friends, this isn't Christianity. Sadly, it's the version of Christianity to which many people subscribe. Our churches are filled on Sunday mornings with members whose only decision for Christ all week is to attend that worship service. Once that box is checked, it's time to enjoy oneself the rest of the week.

We live in a world today where the believer doesn't look all that different from the nonbeliever. As a matter of fact, it is very hard to tell at times whether someone is a Christ-follower or not. Actually, I need to correct that last sentence. If someone is truly a Christ-follower, they are easy to spot. They act different, many times look different, and certainly carry themselves in a different way. A person who has truly given their life to Christ and is allowing his spirit to lead and guide their life sticks out like a sore thumb in this broken, sinful world. This leads me then to the only possible conclusion—many people who profess to be followers of Jesus Christ are not really saved. They are lost.

Now before you get upset with me, let's go back to the scriptures to see what a committed Christ-follower looks like. Let's start with Paul. Paul, the great missionary, actually got his start as Saul, the enemy of Christianity. He dedicated his early life to killing Christians and stopping the spread of what he saw as a heretical belief. Saul literally went from city to city terrorizing the early church. He was present and pleased when a man named Stephen was stoned to death for preaching the Gospel. Then, it happened. An encounter with Jesus changed everything.

Acts 9 tells us his story. While traveling down the road, Saul was stopped in his tracks by a flash of light. It literally blinded him for a period. Jesus entered Saul's life and rocked his world. Saul the Christian-hater became Paul the Christ-lover. His life was never the same. The apostle Paul was one of the greatest missionaries in the history of the world. He spent the rest of his life on a mission to spread the Gospel to the ends of the earth. His letters make up more than half the New Testament. What changed? Paul became a Christian! Jesus changed everything.

How about Peter? Peter was one of Jesus's twelve closest friends. He spent the better part of several years traveling with Jesus and learning from his ministry. However, when the going got tough and Jesus was about to be crucified, Peter bailed! "I do not know this man!" he claimed over and over to anyone willing to listen. "I am not with Him!" When faced with a life-and-death situation, Peter turned his back on Jesus. His faith was tested, and he failed miserably. But a few days later, everything changed. Again, it was an encounter with Jesus that made the difference.

Peter was an eyewitness to a resurrected Savior. He talked with Jesus after Jesus defeated the grave. He enjoyed a meal with him. He probably even touched the nail-scarred hands. Peter was never the same. From that minute on, he passionately preached the Gospel to anyone willing to listen. He continued to spread the good news even under threat of losing his life. Eventually, Peter himself was crucified for his beliefs. It didn't matter. Peter's faith had become real and could not be shaken. He was a saved man living for a cause much greater than anything else in the world. Peter was a Christian! Jesus had changed everything.

Using Paul and Peter as standards, how sold out and committed are you to your faith? I am not talking about limiting your alcohol intake on Friday and Saturday night, dropping a twenty in the offering plate on Sunday, and not committing murder Monday through Thursday. While those may all be good things, they do not make you a Christ-follower. True Christianity is an authentic, ongoing relationship with the King of Kings and Lord of Lords. It is a burning desire for your life to count for something in God's kingdom. It is a complete and total surrender of every area of your life to the One who can be trusted to lead the way.

Surrendering to WIN

In Revelation there is a passage written to the church at Laodicea. Verses 15 and 16 of chapter 3 have this to say: "I know your deeds, that you are neither cold nor hot. I wish you were either one or the other! So, because you are lukewarm—neither hot nor cold—I am about to spit you out of my mouth." Ouch! I don't know about you, but I do not wish to be spit out of the mouth of God. The things we spit out of our mouths are undesirable, distasteful, or rotten. Is that the way God views you? Is that the way he views me? I sure hope not! Yet this scripture is clearly telling us that God doesn't appreciate our lukewarm approach to him.

Pastor Francis Chan, in his best-selling book *Crazy Love*, goes as far as to say that this picture in Revelation of a lukewarm person is a picture of someone who isn't really a Christian at all. According to Chan, "a lukewarm Christian is an oxymoron; there's no such thing. To put it plainly, churchgoers who are lukewarm are not Christians. We will not see them in Heaven."[1] I have to say I agree. It is difficult for my brain to comprehend how someone can come face-to-face with the God of the Bible and the transforming power of this Gospel message and not be on fire for him. Like lukewarm coffee that has been zapped on high for a few minutes in the microwave, so should we warm up quickly when his spirit enters our hearts. It is not my intent to cause you to doubt your salvation. I recognize that there are Christ-followers who struggle with habitual sin and do not live a victorious life. However, my personal conviction is that those who have little desire for God and continue on a path of sin with no remorse do not have a true relationship with Jesus. Pastor Chan challenges us to ask these questions of ourselves: "Has my relationship with Jesus changed the way I live? Am I totally in love with Jesus or would the words half-hearted, lukewarm, or partially committed be a better descriptor of me? Is there evidence of God's Kingdom in my life?"

---

1 Francis Chan, *Crazy Love* (Colorado Springs, Colorado: David C. Cook, 2008).

THE GREATEST STEWARDSHIP

Pastor Larry Stege is a dear friend of mine and currently serves on staff at our church. For many years, he has counseled married couples as a part of his ministry. When he meets with the couple for the first time, he doesn't start out by asking about the marriage. He asks a very simple question and directs it at both the husband and the wife: Are you saved?

Larry says that 100 percent of the time both the husband and the wife initially answer yes. He then takes a few minutes to explain what it means to truly be an authentic Christ-follower. His explanation includes the following five points:

1) Authentic Christ-followers enjoy daily communication with God. This includes daily prayer to speak with God and daily Bible reading to hear from God. An authentic Christian has a deep desire to know God better and have fellowship with him.

2) Authentic Christ-followers want to be around other true believers. As the old saying goes, "Birds of a feather flock together." The main place Christians find community and godly fellowship is by being active in a local church. An authentic Christian attends regularly, worships wholeheartedly, and serves faithfully at their place of worship.

3) Authentic Christ-followers are generous givers. They understand that God is the owner of all things and they are simply managers of his resources. With this principle as their guide, authentic Christians step up when needs are brought to their attention. Authentic Christians are also faithful givers to the church and understand that tithing is a starting point, not a finish line.

4) Authentic Christ-followers share their faith. Like a patron who has found a good restaurant or a patient who has been made well by a good medicine, we share

good news when it happens to us! Authentic Christians are so excited about what Jesus has done in their life they cannot help but share it with others.

5) Authentic Christ-followers produce good fruit. The Bible tells us that Christians will be known by their fruit. A bad tree produces bad fruit, but good fruit is the result when a tree is good and healthy. The fruits of the spirit are love, joy, peace, patience, kindness, goodness, faithfulness, gentleness, and self-control. Authentic Christians' lives are characterized by these positive qualities.

After walking the couple through these attributes of an authentic Christ-follower, Larry again asks the question—based on what I've just shared with you, are you saved? Only 50 percent of women still say yes, and only 30 percent of men still say yes. Larry says the reason he asks these questions is not to tell someone they are saved or lost. He simply wants them to do what Paul teaches us to do and examine themselves to see if they are in the faith.

So, before I move on, I would like for you to prayerfully "examine yourself" after considering what you have just read. Are you truly saved? Are you a committed Christ-follower? Here is the reality. Jesus as Savior and Jesus as Lord are inseparable. He is either both in your life or neither. Think about it this way: when you ask Jesus to save you and when you accept his work on the cross as payment for your sins, you are also surrendering to him as Lord of your life. With salvation comes a new creation. The new creation is prepared to follow Jesus as Lord in every area of your life. You cannot have one without the other. Pastor Craig Groeschel uses the term "Christian atheist" to describe people who say they believe in God but live as though he doesn't exist.

The Gospel is either true or it is not. God's redemptive plan of salvation, as we discussed in the previous chapters, is either the way or the lie. At some point in everyone's life, we face the most important decision we will ever make: Do I believe or not? Am I willing to stake my eternity on God's truths, or will I continue blazing my own trail? Am I willing to live this life according to a belief system that requires me to go in the opposite direction of the world? Here is what I want you to consider: If you are truly surrendered to Christ and have made him Lord of your life, everything changes. Everything. He is either Lord of all in your life or not Lord at all. There is no middle ground.

If the spirit of the one true God resides in you and directs your path, you are no longer the same person you were before salvation. You are now a child of the King. You have been bought by the precious blood of the Lamb. Your life now overflows with joy, hope, and love. You are set apart and called to a greater purpose than our feeble minds could ever dream up. Friends, this truth should rock your world! It should cause you to wake up every day on fire for the Lord. We should embrace every ounce of time and energy God gives us and seek to glorify him with it. We should no longer be difficult to pick out from a crowd of nonbelievers. Again, Jesus changes everything! Our victory is found in him and because of him.

We have established the fact that followers of Jesus are not simply people who have walked an aisle, been baptized, or added their name to a church roll. Born-again believers are those people who have turned from their sins and truly given their lives to Christ. They are living life on a mission from God. Like Jesus stated when he was lost from his parents at the temple, they are "all about their Father's business." So what exactly does "being about the Father's business" look like? I will give you three things:

1) To be on a mission for Christ and take care of the business we are called to do, we must first understand the mission and the "family business." This is summed up nicely for us in Matthew 28:19 in what has become

known as the great commission. "Go and make disciples of all nations, baptizing them in the name of the Father, Son, and Holy Spirit, teaching them to observe all things I have commanded you, and surely I am with you always to the very end of the age." I've heard this verse preached and quoted my whole life. I probably had it memorized by the time I was six. But a few years ago, God revealed to me the magnitude of what Jesus was saying here.

Let's start with a little background information. Jesus, the Son of God, came to earth and started a ministry. For thirty-three years, he walked this very earth and preached about a new way and a new kingdom. His teachings made some people so angry that leaders and rulers conspired to kill him. But that didn't faze him in the least. In the face of imminent death, he continued to proclaim the great news of forgiveness, freedom, and salvation. Ultimately, this cost him his life. Then, God raised him from the dead three days later, defeating death, hell, and the grave once and for all. Before he went back to his throne in heaven, he stopped by to say hello to some old friends. And just before he ascended up to heaven to be reunited with his Father, he gave us the words of Matthew 28:19. Go, make disciples, baptize, and teach.

Think for a second about everything I just said. Let the incredible weight of the responsibility of what you just read sink in. Jesus, before leaving this world and ending his own personal ministry, gave you and me the responsibility of continuing what he started. Talk about stewardship! Wow! He entrusted us with this powerful Gospel message and commanded us to take it to every nation. His plan for the spread of his message was to use people like you and me. This rocked the disciples' worlds. It should rock ours too!

If what I have just said smacked you in the face, you now understand why a Christ-follower should be easy to spot. Our light should shine brighter, and our salt should be stronger. We are on a mission from God. It is not optional. It is the greatest privilege yet the greatest responsibility we have. The best news anyone could ever hear has been entrusted to us to reach a hopeless world. It is the ultimate stewardship. It's time we begin taking this responsibility seriously.

2) If our mission is for Christ in response to his command, we need to learn as much as we can about him. We must desire to know him in the deepest possible way. We must strengthen our relationship with him every day. This is accomplished through Bible study and prayer. Fortunately, we have everything we need because he reveals himself to us over and over in his word. And because of Jesus's great sacrifice on the cross, the communication lines from here to heaven are now open. Daily prayer and Bible study should be a part of every Christ-follower's life.

I'm not talking about in a legalistic, check-the-box manner. I'm talking about getting alone with God and connecting with him in a truly meaningful way. Talking to God and listening to what he is saying back to you. Studying his word with a goal of learning about him and his commands for your life. Hungering for that sweet fellowship that comes when you get still and quiet and just meditate on a holy God.

In Exodus 34 Moses's face literally became radiant when he spent time with the Lord on Mount Sinai. It was glowing! His time with the Lord caused such a positive reaction that he had to cover his face while delivering instruction to Aaron and the Israelites. Oh, may we also experience such positive interactions with our Lord!

I struggled with this for years after I gave my life to Christ. I tried different ways to study the Bible and pray, but nothing seemed to work. Because of the way I'm wired, this time in my day was simply another item added to my checklist. One chapter of the Bible—check. A two-minute prayer—check. Fifteen minutes of sitting quietly meditating on God—no check. That one usually got left blank. The minute I would sit down, all the activities of the day would flood my brain. No matter how hard I tried, I struggled to focus on God. For years I also carried guilt because I felt like I wasn't a good person since I didn't really get a lot out of Bible study and quiet time. Over the years, that slowly changed. Actually my heart is what changed first. I had been prioritizing the other activities in my day over the most important one. When God changed my heart and showed me what was truly important, my desires changed. Then new actions followed my new heart. When I finally grasped the magnitude of the "Father's business," my desire to know him skyrocketed.

3) We can understand our life's mission and spend time getting to know the mission-maker, but if we do not obey, we will not be effective. In our quest to be on a mission for God and have a significant kingdom impact, disobedience might be the biggest obstacle. God's word is very clear on most things. Sex before marriage—sin. Drunkenness—sin. Gossip—sin. Murder—sin. Pride—sin. Laziness—sin. The list goes on and on. We were

born sinners. All have sinned and fallen short of the glory of God. When Adam and Eve ate the forbidden fruit, there were consequences. Cain killed Abel. He sinned and faced consequences. David had sex with Bathsheba and then had her husband killed. David's sins led to the death of his son and many other negative consequences.

When we disobey God, it leads to bad things. We cannot be all that God wants us to be when we are living in sin. If we are going to be effective in fulfilling the great commission, we must repent of our sins and turn from our wicked ways. We must strive to obey God. Notice I used the word "strive." Perfection isn't possible for us. In this broken world, we are going to stub our toe every now and then. That's why Christ came. He paid a price we could not pay so that we could have complete and total forgiveness of our sins. However, we shouldn't use the fact that we live in a sinful, broken world as an excuse. Our lives should be characterized by radical obedience and repentance. When we are living in obedience and running away from a life of sin, God can use us. That's when our lives as Christ-followers can thrive in this great mission God has called us to. Remember, "Our job is obedience. His job is everything else."

This life-changing Gospel message caught fire during the life of Jesus and continues to this day. Billions of people across the globe have believed and given their lives to Christ. I am thankful for men like Paul who stewarded the Gospel message so well. He took seriously his responsibility to share the love of Christ and spread the message of salvation. Friends, we have the same responsibility and the same opportunity. The great commission applies to us as Christ-followers just as much as it did to Paul and Peter. And your pastor. And your friend who is on the mission field. Ask yourself this question: What have I done with this powerful Gospel message that has been entrusted to me? If you have surrendered your life to Christ, the next step is living for him according to his commands.

Following Christ isn't just another thing to add to your already busy schedule. It is the *only* thing that matters. When the transforming truth of the Gospel and great commission truly penetrates your head and your heart, you will never be the same. Every single part of your life is like spokes on a bicycle revolving around the hub that is Jesus. His influence in your life should change the way you talk, act, think, and work. He should change your attitude and your actions. He should completely change your heart. And when this happens, no one will have to ask if you are saved. The Bible says we will know them by their fruit. Your fruit will tell the world all they need to know. Follow him. Surrender everything to Jesus and pursue him with all you have. Embrace this incredible stewardship opportunity we've been given to be his witnesses in a lost world.

Consider the words of this powerful poem, "My Friend," from the book *One Thing You Can't Do in Heaven*:

> My friend I stand in judgement now.
> And feel that you're to blame somehow.
> On Earth I walked with you day by day,
> And never did you even point the way.
> You knew the Lord in truth and Glory,
> But never did you tell me the story.
> My knowledge then was very dim,
> You could have led me safely to Him.
> Though we lived together here on Earth.
> You never told me of the second birth.
> And now I stand this day condemned,

THE GREATEST STEWARDSHIP

> Because you failed to mention Him.
> We walked by day and talked by night,
> And yet you showed me not the light.
> You let me live, and love, and die,
> You knew I'd never live on High.
> Yes, I called you friend in life,
> And trusted you through joy and strife.
> And yet as we come to this dreadful end,
> I cannot now call you "my friend."[2]

Who in your life needs to hear about the good news of Jesus Christ? I cringe to think that God placed someone in my sphere of influence who didn't know him, and that I failed to do my part in leading that person to Jesus.

John Harper was someone who stewarded the Gospel message well. In 1912 Harper was traveling to Chicago to take up his appointment as pastor of Moody Church. The ship he was traveling on was the *Titanic*. He had his daughter Nana on board with him. His wife had died a few years earlier. When the *Titanic* struck the iceberg and began to sink, he put Nana into a lifeboat and then ran throughout the ship, yelling, "Women, children, and *unsaved*, get into the lifeboats!" When the ship finally went down, he had already given his life jacket to another passenger. *Survivors report that to the very end Harper was witnessing to anyone who would listen.* One survivor recalls clinging to one of the ship's spars when Harper floated near him. "Man, are you saved?" cried Harper.

"No, I'm not" replied the man.

"Believe in the Lord Jesus Christ, and you shall be saved," pleaded Harper.

The waves carried Harper away and brought him back a little later. "Are you saved now?" asked Harper.

---

[2] Mark Cahill, *One Thing You Can't Do in Heaven* (Rock Wall, Texas: Biblical Discipleship Publishers, 2006).

"No, I cannot honestly say that I am," said the man.

Again, Harper pleaded with him, "Believe in the Lord Jesus Christ, and thou shalt be saved."

Shortly afterward John Harper went down. The man who survived was one of only six people rescued, but in a public meeting four years later, recounting this episode, he said "There, alone in the night, and with two miles of water under me, I believed. I am John Harper's last convert to Christianity."

John Harper modeled for us what it looks like to take seriously our responsibility to share this powerful Gospel message. Oh, may we, too, understand the urgency of getting this good news to a world that is lost and in desperate need of Jesus. This is God's plan for the amazing message of hope that he entrusted to us.

Simple Summary

1) Salvation is more than fire insurance. It's a call to a radically different lifestyle.

2) The Bible is full of examples of changed lives due to an encounter with Jesus.

3) The Gospel is either true or it's not. If it's true, the implications are mind-blowing.

4) We are on a mission from God. His commands to his followers are very clear.

5) When it's all said and done, Jesus is the only thing that matters.

Conclusion

Chapter 15

CREATOR OR CREATION?

*You shall not make for yourself an idol
in the form of anything in heaven above or
on the earth beneath or in the waters below.*
—Exodus 20:4

Before I conclude, it is worth briefly mentioning one of the final barriers of surrender and stewardship. This subtle but powerful challenge we all face is best introduced through a personal story.

Near the home where Aubrey and I lived for the first ten years of our marriage was a house with statues in the backyard. Occasionally we would see the owners of the home out in the yard bowing down and worshipping these idols. Each time I saw this happening, I just shook my head and thought how sad it must be to worship a false god. It almost seemed silly to me. I had read the Ten Commandments hundreds of times and always glazed right over the commandments that mentioned having idols and putting false gods ahead of the one true God. It was difficult to see how this applied to me. At this point, you are probably thinking exactly the way I did. I do not have a golden cow or a bronze statue in my back yard. I am a monotheist, and my God is not made by human hands. As a matter of fact, he is alive and well and rules over the human race.

Surrendering to WIN

As I wrestled with what I was seeing, God convicted me and helped me see these verses in a whole new light. *Anything we give first place in our lives can become an idol.* Let me say that a different way: when we take our eyes off the Creator and begin seeking our ultimate joy and fulfillment from the creation, we are guilty of idolatry. It doesn't have to be a statue made of stone. It can be anything we turn to instead of the one true God. Ouch! So, sports can be an idol? Yes! So, power and success can be idols? Yes! So, money and possession can be idols? Yes! Listen to what Pastor Kyle Idleman wrote about this in his book *Gods at War*: "Idolatry isn't just one of many sins. It's the one great sin that all the others come from. If you start peeling back the layers of whatever you are struggling with, eventually you will find that underneath it is a false god. Until that god is dethroned and God is given his rightful place, you will not experience victory."[1]

Kyle uses the word victory. Again, it seems counterintuitive, but true victory is achieved only by full surrender. We win when we remove other things from the center of our focus and give God his rightful position. God wants first place in our lives. He doesn't want to have to compete with anything for the throne of our hearts. Listen to what he says in Psalm 96:4–5: "For great is the Lord and most worthy of praise; he is to be feared above all gods. For all of the gods of the nations are idols, but the Lord made the Heavens."

Our God is greater. Our God is stronger. Our God is higher than any other. He is worthy to be praised. And he is certainly worthy of our worship. Creator God gives us creation for our enjoyment. But those "little g" gods are temporary. They do not provide lasting joy and fulfillment. Listen to what David Platt had to say in his book *Follow Me*:

---

[1] Kyle Idleman, *Gods at War* (Grand Rapids, Michigan: Zondervan, 2013).

CREATOR OR CREATION?

When we think of worshipping idols and false gods, we often picture Asian people buying carved images of wood, stone, or gold or African tribes performing ritualistic dances around burning sacrifices. But we don't consider the American man looking at pornography, the American woman addicted to shopping or obsessively consumed with the way she looks. We don't take into account men and women who are enamored with money or blindly engulfed in materialism. We hardly even think about our busy efforts to climb the corporate ladder, our worship of sports, our anger and temper when things don't go our way, our constant worrying about things we can't control, our overeating, and all our other excesses. We can't fathom someone on the other side of the world believing that a wooden god can save them, but we have no problem believing that money, possessions, food, fame, sex, sports, status, and success can satisfy us.[2]

We must be very careful not to surrender to the wrong god. Here is a good self-reflection question to ask: What are some common idols that battle for the throne of your heart? Said another way, what are two or three things that are currently hindering your walk with God and keeping you from living a fully surrendered life? Hebrews 12:1–2 tells us to "throw off everything that hinders us and the sin that so easily entangles us and let us run with perseverance the race marked out for us. Let us fix our eyes on Jesus the author and perfecter of our faith." Focus on Jesus. Keep your eyes on the Creator. Surrender to him and him alone. Do not allow your heart's affection to be divided among other gods. To bring more clarity to this concept, we are going to examine three of the most common "little g" gods we are guilty of worshipping.

---

[2] David Platt, *Follow Me* (Carol Stream, Illinois: Tyndale House Publishers, 2013).

Surrendering to WIN

Sports

Be forewarned that what follows could very likely step on your toes. It stepped on mine. But it needs to be said. We are obsessed with sports in the United States of America. Before you stop reading or your defenses go up, consider the following story. Unfortunately, you will need to use your imagination.

It is Monday morning. There is a major press conference scheduled at your church. All the major news outlets have sent reporters to cover it. At this press conference, the schedule of your pastor's upcoming sermons will be announced. Also, the worship music for next Sunday's service will be released. Your church's ticket office sells out of tickets within a few minutes of the press conference's conclusion. Ticket prices are over $100 each. After the sanctuary is completely sold out, tickets hit the secondary market for over $500 per ticket. The seats on the front pews go for $1,700. Parking passes also sell out quickly because members do not want to walk very far to get inside the building. Those only go for $50 apiece. Sunday arrives, and the streets leading to your church are rerouted to aid traffic flow. Service starts at 11:00 a.m., but people start arriving at 4:00 a.m. The parking lot is full of people fellowshipping, cooking hamburgers, and passionately discussing the events to come. Christian music is blaring through speakers everywhere. When the church staff arrive, they are led by police escorts through the screaming fans and into the building. Matt Chandler, David Platt, and Andy Stanley have a stage set up in the grass by the church to discuss this service as well as all the worship services across the country. During the service, everyone is standing, cheering, worshipping, and praising the risen Savior. After the service is over, people hang around for hours to discuss what has just taken place. It is also discussed for weeks on television, radio talk shows, and around every watercooler in America. Several other churches contact your pastor and try to recruit him to a vacant position. However, your deacons and finance committee will have none of that. They quickly meet and offer to raise his salary to $5 million per year.

Doesn't that sound crazy? It should actually sound quite familiar, because it is something that happens often in our country. Every Saturday and Sunday from September to February, this takes place in football stadiums everywhere. Hundreds of millions of people flock to massive stadiums to be entertained by a game. Pro football is now a $15 billion industry. Is there anything wrong with football? No. In its place, it is a great form of family entertainment. However, I believe we have made it an idol. I am ashamed to admit the number of times my worship suffered on Sunday morning because my team had lost on Saturday night.

I have seen grown men get into fist fights at football games. I have seen church members fall out with each other over the result of a rivalry game. And I have seen sports slowly but surely move into spots on our schedule that used to be designated for worship services. The baseball and soccer fields are now covered on Sunday mornings with children who need to hear about Jesus. We must be very careful not to allow a game to take over our minds and hearts. This is a classic example of letting the creation become more important than the Creator.

Money and Possessions

We've already touched on biblical stewardship as it relates to our money. So consider this a warning of the power money and possessions can have over us if we let them. According to the *Christian Post*, a survey was conducted asking people what they would be willing to do for $10 million. The results will blow your mind (I hope!):

- Twenty-five percent would completely abandon their family.

- Twenty-three percent would quit their job and be a prostitute.
- Sixteen percent would give up their American citizenship.
- Seven percent would murder a total stranger if they knew they wouldn't end up in jail.
- Three percent would put kids up for adoption.[3]

Are you kidding me? Don't tell me the love of money is not a problem. Somehow, we have bought into the false assumption that more money will solve all our problems. This is a lie the enemy wants us to believe. If he can get us to place our faith and trust in stuff, we will never be satisfied. Ecclesiastes 5:10 speaks directly to this: "Whoever loves money never has enough; whoever loves wealth is never satisfied with their income. This too is meaningless."

Money is a false god. It is simply a tool to be used during the short time we are here on earth. So why do we struggle with this so much? Because there isn't a single aspect of our lives that isn't impacted by money. And when we are struggling with it, the effect is tremendous. It affects our prayer life and our quiet time. It affects our work performance and our relationships. And it increases stress and worry in our lives. Let me remind you again that Jesus said we cannot serve two masters. We must choose between God and money. We must master our money, or it will master us.

Ourselves

Yes, you read that heading right. If we are not careful, we will make our own lives and our own well-being an idol. Former professional football player Terrell Owens summed up our selfish

---

[3] Jerry Newcombe, "What Would You Do for $10,000,000?" (*Christian Post*, June 20, 2013).

nature when he said in an interview, "I love me some me!" The rest of us may not say it, but we feel the same way. At the core of who we are, we reek of selfishness. When my boys were really young, it was very common to hear, "I want it! I want it! I want it! No, I had it first! It's mine! It's mine!" We are born that way and unfortunately find it difficult to change. So, what is at the root of this selfishness? I believe the answer is pride. Pride makes us want everything to be about us. Pride causes us to want to steal the spotlight from others. Pride is the true root of most sins. The Bible tells us that Jesus literally "opposes the proud." That one verse alone should awaken us to the dangers of living a selfish, prideful life.

How do you remove yourself from the throne of your own heart? The answer is serving others. Jesus modeled this for us during his time on earth. He said in Matthew 20:28, "The Son of Man did not come to be served but to serve and to give his life as a ransom for many." Serving others helps us stay humble and focused on something (or someone) other than ourselves. Philippians 2:3–4 tells us to "Do nothing out of selfish ambition or vain conceit, but in humility consider others as better than yourselves. Each of you should look not only to your own interests, but also to the interests of others." As we serve others and put their interests ahead of our own, our heart begins to be transformed. There is deep inner joy found in serving others. But it not only takes a transformed heart. It also takes a fully surrendered heart. Keep in mind: We are the creation. He is the Creator. Focusing on ourselves causes our hearts to seek the wrong things. Focusing on Jesus results in love being poured out on those around us. The surrendered heart lets Jesus destroy pride and selfishness.

Unfortunately, I write from personal experience on this topic. First of all, I am a recovering legalist. By my very nature I am performance-driven, so a legalistic version of faith came naturally to me. Over the years I have surrendered this performance idol to God and embraced his grace-based Gospel. Second, I have allowed several things to rule over my heart (in place of Jesus) in the past. It started with my basketball career. In my younger days, I was very successful and thought I was surely NBA material. So basketball became my god. I obsessed about it for years and allowed it to hinder my relationship with the Lord. As I grew older, I developed an unhealthy obsession with money. I wanted to get rich quick, retire early, and live the American dream. Ironically, God turned this money idol in my life into a ministry opportunity. When I finally surrendered and released my grip on the almighty dollar, God called me into the ministry of money. Today I spend most of my working hours helping people win in an area I used to struggle with. God is good! And when we give him first place in our lives, we, too, can be victorious.

In this life there will be many potential idols you will have to defeat. As Larry Burkett stated, "When we surrender every area of our lives—including our finances—to God, then we are free to trust Him to meet our needs. But if we would rather hold tightly to those things that we possess, then we find ourselves in bondage to those very things." I believe the universal remedy for defeating all idols is found in Romans 1:25: "They exchanged the truth about God for a lie and worshipped and served *created things rather than the Creator*—who is forever praised." When we worship things created instead of the Creator of all things, idols begin to form. But when we worship the Creator, something magical happens. It is summed up in the old hymn "Turn Your Eyes upon Jesus." This is what happens when we focus on the Creator and not creation: "The things of this earth grow strangely dim in the light of His glory and grace."

Oh, may we all keep our eyes on the Creator so that sports, sex, power, possessions, careers, money, social media, acceptance, and all other idols take a back seat to the one true God. We simply cannot be surrendered to God and be faithful life stewards if

CREATOR OR CREATION?

our loyalties are split between Jesus and mammon. My prayer for myself and for each of you is that those things grow strangely dim as we surrender our hearts and worship the King of Kings, Lord of Lords, and the God of Gods.

Simple Summary

1) Idols are anything that competes with Jesus for the thrones of our hearts.

2) Our country has an unhealthy obsession with sports. It many ways sports has become an idol.

3) Many times we give money and possessions first place in our lives.

4) We must also be careful not to worship ourselves and our own selfish desires.

5) We can achieve victory over idolatry by focusing on the Creator and not the creation.

WRAP-UP

So what does all this look like practically when lived out in our daily lives? If you want a simple formula, it is *pray and obey*. When you pray and obey, it is easier to accept outcomes. Why? Because it is very likely you are centered in the will of God and whatever is going on is part of his plan, even if it's difficult to understand. But when we fail to communicate with our Heavenly Father and are disobedient to his commands, our lives take a detour. We have taken over the driver's seat and are likely to end up in a ditch.

A few years back, I became obsessed with knowing exactly what God's will was for my life. I didn't want to miss it. Was he calling me into full-time ministry? Was I doing enough for his kingdom? Was there someone I needed to help or something I needed to do that I had overlooked? The Bible verse that states to whom much is given much is required haunted me. I knew I had been richly blessed. Was I stewarding these blessings well? There are very few things that keep me awake at night. This was one of those things. I truly wanted to be in the center of God's will for my life. It was during that time a mentor of mine shared two things with me I'll never forget. These truths gave me complete peace about my calling and the journey I was on:

1) God wants us to know his plan for us. He doesn't try to hide it and make us guess what he is up to in our lives. Like a great father who leads and guides his children, so it is with God. His word tells us when we seek him with all our heart, we will find him. His spirit is

there to guide us every step of the way. And when we are unsure about which path to take? God can work all things together for good. Nothing surprises him. As long as we aren't violating scripture, God can bless whichever path we choose.

2) Surrender and obedience are critical. His word is very clear on what is right and what is wrong. When we surrender every day to him and obey his commands, he leads us to exactly the place in life to which he wants us to go. It's just that simple! I don't have to worry about tomorrow or next week or next year. Just surrender today. Obey today. And if I do that consistently over time, I end up right where God wants me to be! This one truth had a profound impact on my life. It really took away a lot of the unnecessary pressure I was placing on myself. Surrender and stewardship are very freeing when done according to God's word.

We must, however, be intentional if we want to live our lives as surrendered faithful stewards. It doesn't just naturally happen. There are some great questions you can ask yourself each day to center your life around these principles.

1) What does obedience look like for me today? Think about your tasks, appointments, and decisions, and carefully think through what God wants from you each day.

2) How can I use (fill in the blank) to bring glory to God? If God has blessed you with a nice house, use it to host church events. If God has given you free time each week, use it for kingdom work. If God has blessed you financially, look for ways to invest in the work God is doing all around you. You get the picture. This applies to everything God has entrusted to us.

CREATOR OR CREATION?

3) How can I use what God has given me to bless (fill in a name) and show them the love of Christ? Think about who will step into your path today. If you begin to view them as a person created in the image of God with their own set of hopes and dreams, your eyes will be open to many ways you can be a blessing.

As I wrestled with these daily surrender and biblical stewardship truths, my next question was how this "strategy" lined up with goal setting. I am a planner. I like to set goals, and I find satisfaction in meeting these goals. The answer came from Proverbs 16:9: "In his heart a man plans his course but the Lord determines his steps." There is nothing wrong with having goals for our future. Personally, I think it's very healthy to have some direction in our lives. But we must remain flexible and allow God to intervene whenever he wants to. This is the essence of surrender. He is in control, not me. His plans are far more important than mine. When he shows me the way he wants me to go, my way has just become a lot less important.

If you don't believe God is in control, ask yourself this question: Fifteen years ago did you see yourself living where you are currently living, doing what you are currently doing, with the spouse or children you currently have? I think we would all say our lives haven't turned out exactly as we thought they would. God probably sits back and smiles when we start planning what our next twenty years will look like.

Prayer is the key to staying in the will of God. We must go before him daily and seek direction for each day. Prayer helps us to acknowledge his authority in our lives. It also allows us to tap into his power, which is critical for winning our daily battles. Without prayer, it is virtually impossible to live the surrendered life. As Pastor Adrian Rogers once said, "Your spiritual life can never rise above your prayer life."

Surrendering to WIN

Consider this prayer written by Scott Rodin. He sums up beautifully the heart, attitude, and posture of a surrendered, faithful steward.

> Lord, as I look across the totality of my life—every second and every hour, every relationship and every love, every thought and every desire, every dollar and every doubt, every fear and every hope—I proclaim that it's all yours! All of it!
>
> Lord, my health is yours, it is not mine. It never was. I surrender it fully into your hands, trusting you to be the great physician in my life. I surrender any anxiety I may have, and I will find my peace in your love and provision.
>
> Lord, my work is yours, it is not mine. It never was. Every day that I work is a gift from you. I have trusted you in the past with my livelihood and I will trust you now. You know my need, you know my desire to work in a meaningful way, to earn a living and support myself and my family. I trust you to meet my need, to engage my hands in the work you have prepared for me. I will wait patiently secure in your loving kindness and sustaining will for my life at work. I trust you Lord, and I will remain confident in your providential care.
>
> Lord, my finances are yours, they are not mine. They never were. You have provided for me in abundance, and regardless of how my bank account or investment portfolio looks today, you are the same faithful God yesterday, today, and forever. You promise you'll never leave me or forsake me, and I lean into that blessed assurance every minute of this day. You know my need, and that is enough for me. Lord, I rest sheltered in you as my sole source of security.
>
> Lord, my future is yours, it is not mine. It never was. As hard as I work to plan everything out and set a clear

course from my life, these days have shown me that I have no final control over anything. I pray that you would help that truth become a source of freedom in my life. Help me exchange my desire to control my future for the joyful surrender of a steward, looking to you to guide me down the path you've chosen for me. Lord, the future is yours and I claim that affirmation as a source of freedom and joy as I steward every minute of it on my journey.

Lord, my life is yours, it is not mine. It never was. You gave me life from the moment I was conceived, you've sustained me with every breath, and you will take me home at exactly the moment you've prepared for me, not a minute too soon or too late. Until then, every day is a gift, my life is a gift and I treasure it and thank you for it. In your ledger, not a minute is wasted. My life counts because it is your gift to me, now help me to make it our gift to others. Lord, let me not fear one second for my life, but invest it lavishly in worship to you and service to my neighbor. And grant me your deep peace until I meet you face-to-face, when I will be eternally, truly, fully yours.

Amen.[4]

What a powerful prayer! God has a plan for our lives. When we are fully surrendered to it, stewardship becomes our natural response. We see time differently. We see our money differently. We see our most important relationships differently. We are just passing through this broken world. Our eternal home is in heaven. While we are here, God gives us various responsibilities. He entrusts his creation to our care. It still belongs to him, but we get to manage it according to his instructions. Just like someone else managed it before we got here, someone else will manage it when

---

4 Scott Rodin, *The Steward's Journey.*

we are gone. That is why we are to do what John Wesley challenged us to do: "Do all the good you can, in all the ways you can, for as many people as you can, and for just as long as you can."

So what is the result of a surrendered life? Victory! We win—not because of what we can do, but because of what he did. When Jesus takes over our lives, we now have great purpose and can find joy in whatever comes our way.

What changes in our lives when we take up a steward's mentality instead of an owner's mentality? Everything! Our stress goes down, and our peace goes up. We release our grip on not just money and possessions but also the direction of our lives. Hear the words of John Wesley when someone frantically told him his house was on fire and was about to burn to the ground. John peacefully replied, "That's not my house. God owns that house. If it is burning down that is one less responsibility God wants me to have."

Paul tells us in Ephesians 3:20 that there is one who is "able to do immeasurably more than all we ask or imagine, according to His power that is at work within us." Here is what almighty God wants to do for us: more than we can even measure! More than we could even ask or imagine! Because of his power, not ours! His power within us! Wow! I don't know about you, but I get excited about the possibilities here. When we surrender to God and surrender to biblical stewardship, our minds cannot comprehend what God can do in and through us. We have no idea what God plans to do with our lives. Great things await us. Our surrendered future includes immeasurably more than we could ask or imagine.

Unfortunately, we will never experience those things if we try to retain all control. We must let go and let God take the reins. Chris Tomlin tells the story of being a broke worship leader from a small town in Texas. He was in his apartment reading his Bible when these words proceeded from his mouth: "how great is our

CREATOR OR CREATION?

God." He started singing these lyrics when other words popped in his head: "the splendor of a king, clothed in majesty." Before that night was over, his best-selling hit "How Great Is Our God" was born. Chris said little did he know that song would launch a successful music career. It quickly reached number one on the charts, and he has now sung it in over twenty countries in twenty different languages! Immeasurably more…than we could ask or imagine…His power…not ours.

There is a character in the Bible who stood in the center of the most pivotal moment in the history of the world. His name was Pontius Pilate, and he was the governor of Judaea. After Jesus had been arrested and beaten, he was brought to Pilate for his final judgment. The Roman soldiers wanted him dead. The chief priests and the elders wanted him dead. The crowds wanted him dead. But Pilate was struggling with this decision. He was amazed at Jesus's lack of fight. He was struggling to find any fault in Jesus of Nazareth. Even Pilate's own wife was concerned and warned her husband to be very careful.

So there Pilate stood with a massive decision on his hands. Should he do what he felt was right and release Jesus? This would make him wildly unpopular. Or should he cave in to the demands of his followers and have Jesus put to death? He chose the latter. His popularity meant more to him than doing the right thing. Pilate agreed to release a notorious prisoner named Barabbas instead of Jesus. Pilate then stood before the crowd and asked one of the most important questions ever asked. "What shall I do then with Jesus who is called Christ?"

You know the rest of the story. Jesus was beaten, mocked, and then put to death. We will never have to choose between keeping Jesus alive or killing him. But every single person who walks this great earth will answer Pilate's question for themselves. What are you going to do with this Jesus who is called the Christ? Will you accept him or reject him? Will you live for him or live for

Surrendering to WIN

yourself? Will you surrender to him or try to maintain control yourself? These are tough questions that require answers.

If you have never placed your faith in Jesus Christ, your answer to Pilate's question will determine your eternal destination. If you are a believer in Jesus Christ but your life looks no different than that of a nonbeliever, you must decide whether you are really serious about your faith. Are you willing to fully surrender every area of your life to him? And, finally, for those of you who have been walking with the Lord for a while and growing in your faith, your answer should include complete and total surrender to biblical stewardship. Let go of control. Give everything over to him, and seek to use everything he has entrusted to you to build his kingdom. May God be with you as you wrestle with this all-important question. If you want the correct answer to the "What should you do with Jesus?" question, here it is. Accept him. Believe him. Obey him. Follow him. Surrender everything to him. And manage all that he has entrusted to you according to his instruction manual, the Holy Bible.